Signs
Everywhere

by
Nancy Kelly-Jones
and
Harley Hamilton

Illustrated by
Carolyn B. Norris

Modern Signs Press, Inc.

Copyright © 1981

International Standard Book Number 0-916708-05-5

Library of Congress Number 81-80388

Publisher

Modern Signs Press, Incorporated
P.O. Box 1181
Los Alamitos, CA 90720
310/596-8548, 310/493-4168 V/TDD
FAX 310/795-6614

Cover by Raya Designs

The publisher welcomes your comments and suggestions

Second printing 1996

Printed in the United States of America

Dedicated to the Deaf Community. . . past, present and future.

ACKNOWLEDGEMENTS

Many people have helped us with this collection of signs. We would especially like to thank the Junior N.A.D., Linda Humphries, Irene Kelly, Cathy Morrison, William Neal, Ken Randall, Anna Rinaldi and Sherri Srb for their assistance at various stages of this project.

A very warm and special thanks to Clyde and Sandy for all their support.

Finally, we wish to thank Geri, Es, and Carol for their interest in this project.

Cover illustration by Marcia A. Lawrence.

TABLE OF CONTENTS

PREFACE

This project began as a result of some of my students' viewing photos of Clyde and me in front of other schools for the deaf that we visited while traveling. The children expressed amazement that they were not the only deaf students in the only school for the deaf in America. There were actually other schools—at least one in each state—which meant there were deaf people in other places.

Because of the Public Law 94-142, more and more hearing-impaired students are being mainstreamed in public schools and therefore having none or very little contact with the Deaf Community. I myself grew up unaware of the Deaf Community, believing there would be some magic stage in life when I would become hearing! Many deaf children have the same misconception.

In addition, Social Studies and Current Events require the mention of cities and states—it delights young students to know there are deaf people and deaf communities all over the continent, and the deaf have made a mark on those places, have laid claim to them to the extent of having a sign.

To supply the students with the currently-used signs from deaf communities all over North America and Mexico, I have co-authored this book. No, the Atlanta Area School for the Deaf is not the only deaf school in existence, the deaf do not become hearing, and signs exist—we do not have to invent ones each time we discuss another place, far away from where we live.

KJ

Notes on symbols
‡- Indicates that the sign is formally identical to a sign used to name another person, place or thing. Two such symbols indicate that two signs which are used to name that city are formally identical to two other signs which name persons, places, or things.

★-Indicates the capital of the state.

Note on illustrations and descriptions - All illustrations and descriptions are of signs being made by a right-handed signer.
Blank "Notes" pages are furnished throughout this book to allow convenient addition of other signs.

Capital letters spelled with hyphens in between indicate that these letters are finger-spelled as part of the sign.
Example: S-F

INTRODUCTION

In recent years, researchers have begun to collect signs used in the deaf community. Stokoe, Casterline and Croneberg (1965, 1976) provided much information on the general vocabulary of American Sign Language. Woodward (1980a) and Doughter, Minken, and Rosen (1980) have investigated signs for sexual behavior and Woodward (1980b) has also dealt with signs of drug use. This text will deal with another specific topic area of sign language. It will provide information on signs that name cities in the United States, Canada, and Mexico. Signs for states (U.S.) and provinces (Canada) have also been included.

The signs in this text were collected over a two-year period from deaf people who had been living in the particular geographic area for at least one year. During this two-year period, hearing educators and interpreters were randomly observed or interviewed. These individuals generally appeared unfamiliar with the signs used by deaf people to name cities. Many of the educators and interpreters used on-the-spot invention of a sign if they needed one and were not familiar with signs already in use. Such invention of signs is unnecessary and may only cause problems in communication.

After collecting the initial set of data (see Linguistic Notes) the authors found it interesting that a particular sign may be used to name several different cities. For example, the same sign is used to name Boston, Mass., Brooklyn, Ohio, Berkeley, Ca., Brooklyn, N.Y., Bloomington, Ind., Bloomington, Ill., and Birmingham, Ala.. Homonyms are also fairly common in spoken languages—there is a Rome in Italy, New York, and Georgia. Such formally identical symbols may, at times, allow ambiguity in communication. For example, a world traveler residing in Atlanta, Ga. who says, "I was in Rome recently," might be misunderstood. Similarly, a sign may not indicate which city of many the person is discussing. For this reason, the authors observed how their deaf informants clarified such situations. The following are strategies which were used.

- After the sign for the city, the state's sign was added.
  ex. BOSTON M-A-S-S
  BERKELEY CALIFORNIA
- The city's name was fingerspelled throughout a conversation.
- The city's name was fingerspelled and then signed. Thereafter the sign was used in the conversation.
- The city's name was signed while the signer simultaneously mouthed or spoke the name.
- The English words for the city's name were signed. For example, Clearwater, Fla. was signed CLEAR WATER after which the local sign, C-W, was introduced.

Woodward (1980c) has suggested that signers may show a preference for one or several of these strategies over others. This possibility merits further investigation.

To conclude, the authors would like to point out that this is a purely descriptive text. The signs contained in this text were collected from deaf signers. There may be sign variations used in different communities which are not described here. Readers should verify the signs in this text with members of the deaf community in their own geographic locale.

We would like to thank Lewis Ballard, Robbin Battison, Dennis Cokely, Gerilee Gustason, and James Woodward for comments on earlier versions of this introduction. Any errors are our own.

Comments and suggestions are welcome. These should be addressed to the publisher.

SIGNS EVERYWHERE
c/o Modern Signs Press
Box 1181
Los Alamitos, CA 90720

HJH

UNITED STATES

(AMERICAN SIGNS)

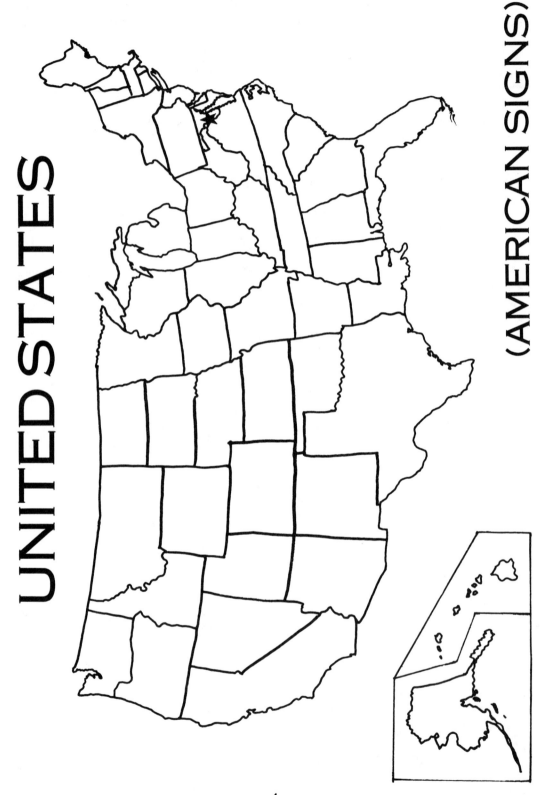

AMERICA

Mesh palm-in fingers, circle horizontally

COUNTRY

Palm-in Y rubs in circle near elbow

CITY, TOWN

Fingertips touch at left; separate; touch at right; "city" may be finger-spelled C-I-T-Y.

STATE

Side of S on fingertips of flat hand arcs down to heel

COMMUNITY

Flat hands, palms in, circle horizontally, tapping.

UNITED STATES

Spell U-S

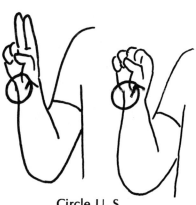

Circle U, S

5

● Huntsville

● Anniston

● Birmingham   ● Talladega

Tuscaloosa ●   ● Sylacauga
           ● Montevallo

● Selma   ★ Montgomery

● Brewton

Mobile ●

ALABAMA

ALABAMA

Spell A-L-A

‡1 **ANNISTON**

A taps side of chest, arcs
to tap other side

3 **BREWTON**

B at chin, then wiggles
down

‡2a **BIRMINGHAM**

B wiggles down

4 **HUNTSVILLE**

Vertical H on palm-left
hand rockets upward

‡2b **BIRMINGHAM**

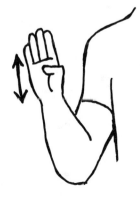

B bobs

5 **MOBILE**

M shakes at ear

6a **MONTEVALLO**

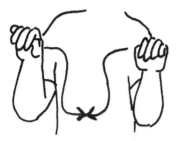

M's move in, then arc
downward to touch

6b **MONTEVALLO**

M on palm-up B circles
upward

‡7 **MONTGOMERY** ★

M circles and touches
temple

‡8 **SELMA**

S wiggles down

‡9 **SYLACAUGA**

Spell S - Y

‡10 **TALLADEGA**

T traces a 7

11a **TUSCALOOSA**

T in palm spirals up

11b **TUSCALOOSA**

Spell T - U - S - C

NOTES

ALASKA

ALASKA

Palm-down A arcs along
forehead to open hand

Barrow

Fairbanks

Anchorage

Juneau

Ketchikan

‡1 ANCHORAGE

A traces a 7

‡2 BARROW

B shakes

4 JUNEAU ★

Spell J-A-U

‡3 FAIRBANKS

F traces a 7

5 KETCHIKAN

K shakes very slightly, then S moves diagonally down and away from the center of the body

ARKANSAS

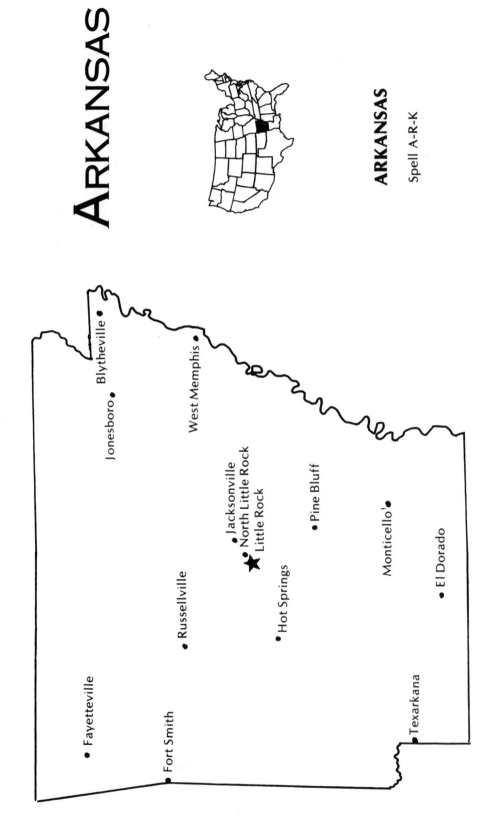

ARKANSAS

Spell A-R-K

Fayetteville

Fort Smith

Russellville

Jonesboro

Blytheville

West Memphis

Jacksonville
North Little Rock
Little Rock

Hot Springs

Pine Bluff

Monticello

El Dorado

Texarkana

1 **BLYTHEVILLE**

Spell B-L -Y

‡2 **EL DORADO**

Spell E-D

3 **FAYETTEVILLE**

Spell F-A-Y

4 **FORT SMITH**

Spell F-S

5 **HOT SPRINGS**

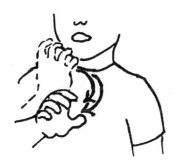

Claw-hand turns out
from open mouth
twice

‡6 **JACKSONVILLE**

Shake J

‡7 **JONESBORO**

Spell J

‡8 **LITTLE ROCK** ★

Spell L-R

9 **MONTICELLO**

Spell M-O-N-T

10 **NORTH LITTLE ROCK**

Spell N-L-R

11 **PINE BLUFF**

Spell P-B

12 **RUSSELLVILLE**

Spell R-U-S-S

13 **TEXARKANA**

Spell T; K traces a 7

14 **WEST MEMPHIS**

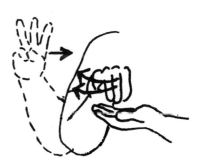

W moves to left,
then M brushes off
palm

ARIZONA

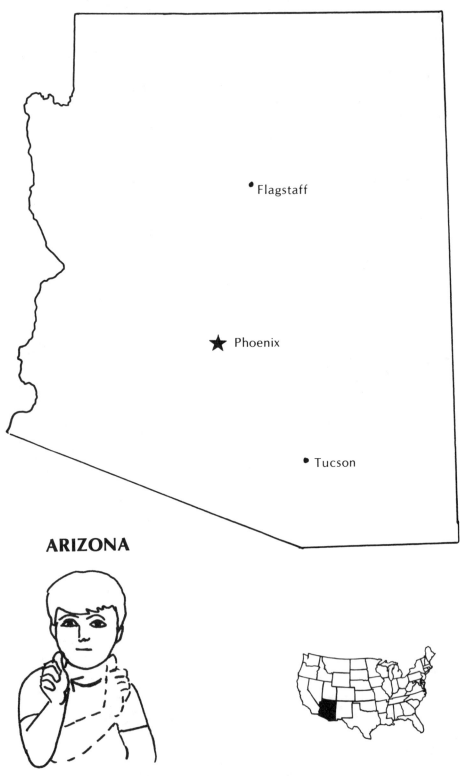

• Flagstaff

★ Phoenix

• Tucson

ARIZONA

A slides down one side
of chin, then the other

14

1 FLAGSTAFF

F-hands, facing, touch
fingertips, repeat
to the side

2 PHOENIX

Shake X

‡3 TUCSON

T traces a 7

CALIFORNIA

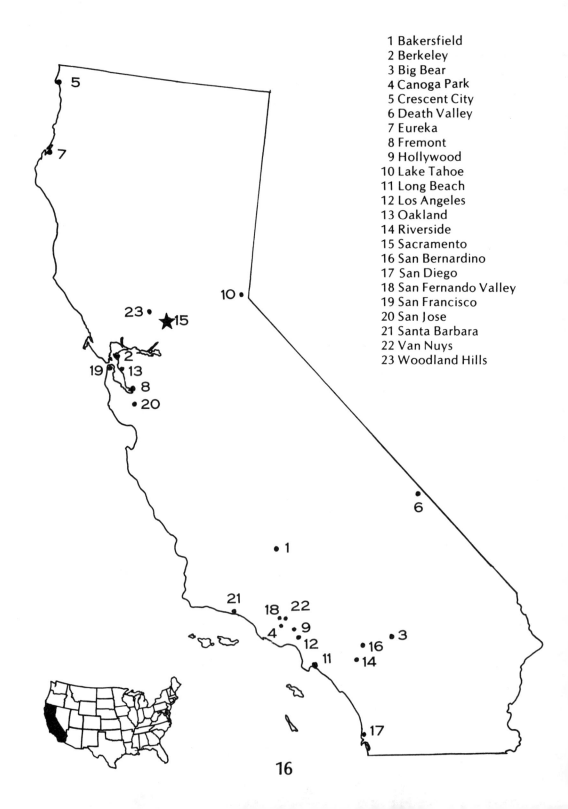

1 Bakersfield
2 Berkeley
3 Big Bear
4 Canoga Park
5 Crescent City
6 Death Valley
7 Eureka
8 Fremont
9 Hollywood
10 Lake Tahoe
11 Long Beach
12 Los Angeles
13 Oakland
14 Riverside
15 Sacramento
16 San Bernardino
17 San Diego
18 San Fernando Valley
19 San Francisco
20 San Jose
21 Santa Barbara
22 Van Nuys
23 Woodland Hills

CALIFORNIA

Open 8-hand shakes to
side from ear

CALIFORNIA

I-L-Y hand shakes to
side from ear

CALIFORNIA

I-L-Y hand shakes to
side from ear, closing
to Y

CALIFORNIA

I-L-Y at ear closes to Y

1   BAKERSFIELD

Spell B-F

‡2   BERKELEY

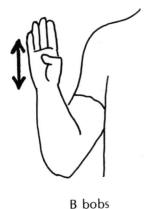

B bobs

‡3a   BIG BEAR

B nods, arcs to right,
nods again

‡3b   BIG BEAR

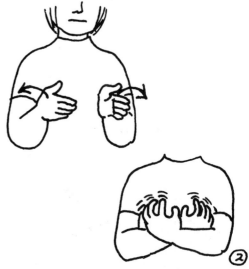

Palm-facing flat hands arc sideways;
cross clawhands and scratch chest

‡4   CANOGA PARK

Spell C-P

‡5   CRESCENT CITY

Nod C, arc to right,
nod again

6 DEATH VALLEY

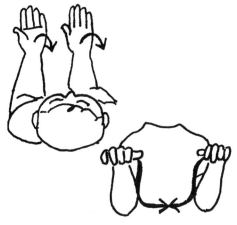

Palms, one facing
down, one up; reverse
position; flat hands
arc down to meet

‡7 EUREKA

E circles

‡8 FREMONT

F bobs

‡9a HOLLYWOOD

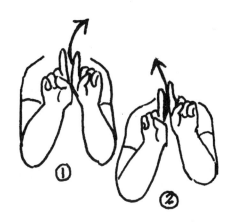

Side of right index
finger strikes upward
against left index
finger; left strikes
against right

9b HOLLYWOOD

Thumbs of 5 hands
alternately touch chest

10 LAKE TAHOE

Spell L-T.

‡11 LONG BEACH

Spell L-B

‡12 LOS ANGELES

Spell L-A

‡13 OAKLAND

O bobs

‡14a RIVERSIDE

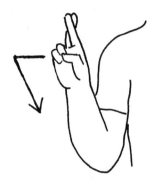

R traces a 7

‡14b RIVERSIDE

R bobs

15 SACRAMENTO ★

Spell S-A-C

16 SAN BERNARDINO

Spell S-B-O

‡17 SAN DIEGO

Spell S-D

18 SAN FERNANDO VALLEY

Spell S-F; flat hands move in, then arc down to touch.

‡19a SAN FRANCISCO

Spell S-F

‡19b SAN FRANCISCO

Together, fingertips of closed F flutter up and down

20 SAN JOSE

Spell S-J

21 SANTA BARBARA

Spell S-B-A

‡22 VAN NUYS

Spell V-N

23 WOODLAND HILLS

Spell W-H

COLORADO

- Fort Collins

- Steamboat Springs

- Boulder

- Denver ★
  - Aurora
  - Englewood

Georgetown •
Glenwood Springs •

- Aspen

- Woodland Park
  - Colorado Springs
  - Manitou Springs

- Pueblo

- Grand Junction

COLORADO

C from shoulder arcs
to elbow, then to wrist

COLORADO

A-D-O

5-hand fingers flutter in
front of mouth, spell
A-D-O

1 **ASPEN**

A-thumbs touch, outline
the shape of an Aspen
leaf

‡2 **AURORA**

Fingertips of right hand
circle once over left palm;
touch mid-palm

‡3 **BOULDER**

Shake B

‡4 **COLORADO SPRINGS**

Spell C-S

‡5a **DENVER**

D bobs

‡5b **DENVER**

D shakes

‡6 **ENGLEWOOD**

Shake E

7 **FORT COLLINS**

Spell F-C

‡8　**GEORGETOWN**

Spell G-T

9a　**GLENWOOD SPRINGS**

Spell G-S

9b　**GLENWOOD SPRINGS**

G-L-E-N-W-O-O-D

Spell G-L-E-N-W-O-O-D; flat O **opens** upward through C to 5; repeat

10　**GRAND JUNCTION**

Spell G-J

11　**MANITOU SPRINGS**

Index, then W touches chin

‡12　**PUEBLO**

Shake P

‡13　**STEAMBOAT SPRINGS**

Open and close S as hand moves to side

‡14　**WOODLAND PARK**

Spell W-P

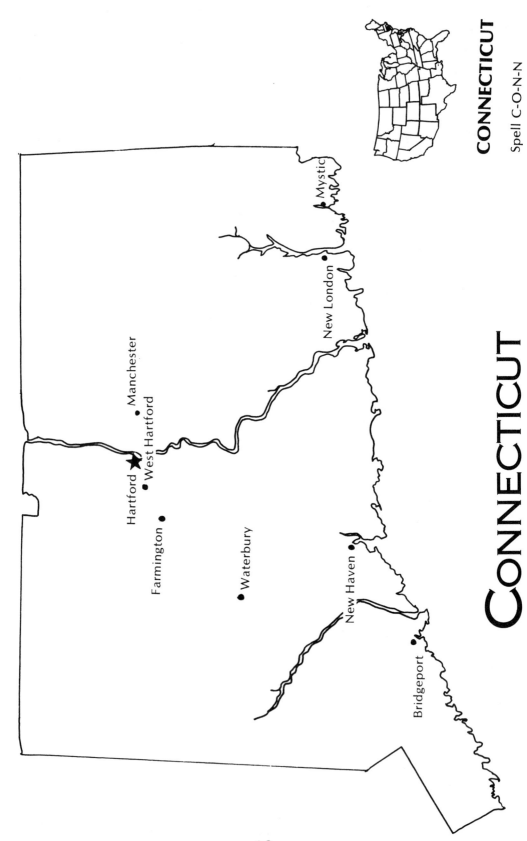

CONNECTICUT

Spell C-O-N-N

CONNECTICUT

Mystic

New London

Manchester

Hartford

West Hartford

Farmington

Waterbury

New Haven

Bridgeport

26

1 BRIDGEPORT

Spell B-P-T

2 FARMINGTON

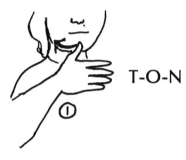

T-O-N

5-hand moves around
chin; spell T-O-N.

‡3 HARTFORD ★

Shake H, palm facing
body

‡4 MANCHESTER

Shake M near jaw

‡5 MYSTIC

Y handshape taps chin
twice

‡6 NEW HAVEN

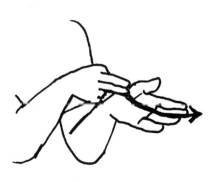

H slides forward on palm-
up hand

7   NEW LONDON

L in palm moves back
and forth

‡9   WEST HARTFORD

Spell W-H

8   WATERBURY

W at chin, then wiggles
down

NOTES

DELAWARE

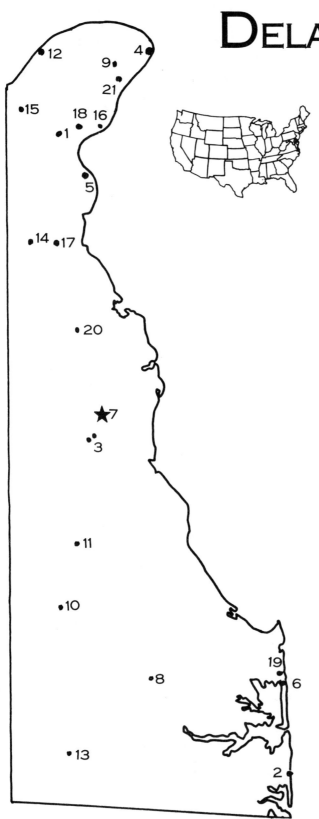

1 Bear
2 Bethany Beach
3 Camden-Wyoming
4 Claymont
5 Delaware City
6 Dewey Beach
7 Dover
8 Georgetown
9 Greenville
10 Greenwood
11 Harrington
12 Hockessin
13 Laurel
14 Middletown
15 Newark
16 New Castle
17 Odessa
18 Ogletown
19 Rehoboth Beach
20 Smyrna
21 Wilmington

DELAWARE

D twists at wrist, inward

‡1 **BEAR**

Cross wrists and scratch chest

5 **DELAWARE CITY**

D-E-L

Spell D-E-L; tap tip of flat hands twice, both circling.

‡2 **BETHANY BEACH**

Nod B, arc to right, nod again

‡6 **DEWEY BEACH**

Spell D-B

‡3 **CAMDEN-WYOMING**

Spell C-W

‡7 **DOVER** ★

‡4 **CLAYMONT**

Shake D

Shake C

31

‡8 **GEORGETOWN**

Spell G-T

9 GREENVILLE

V-I-L-L-E

Shake G; spell V-I-L-L-E

10 GREENWOOD

Spell G-W

‡11 HARRINGTON

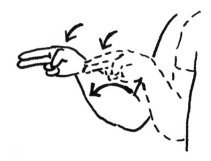

Nod H, arc to right, nod again

12 HOCKESSIN

H palm down, taps heart

‡13 LAUREL

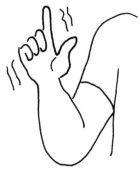

Shake L

14 MIDDLETOWN

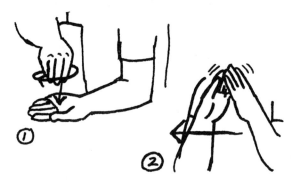

Bent hand circles and touches palm; then 5-fingertips touch, moving to side

‡15 NEWARK

Shake N

‡16a NEW CASTLE

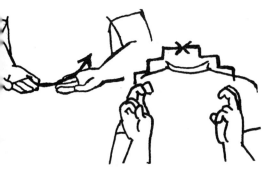

Palm-up right hand arcs down, brushes across left palm, and arcs up slightly; bent V's move in steplike fashion toward each other

‡16b NEW CASTLE

Spell N-C

‡17 ODESSA

Shake O

‡18 OGLETOWN

O approaches and touches left index

19 REHOBOTH BEACH

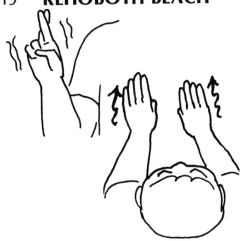

Shake R; palm-down flat hands ripple forward left

‡20 SMYRNA

Shake S

‡21 WILMINGTON

W bobs

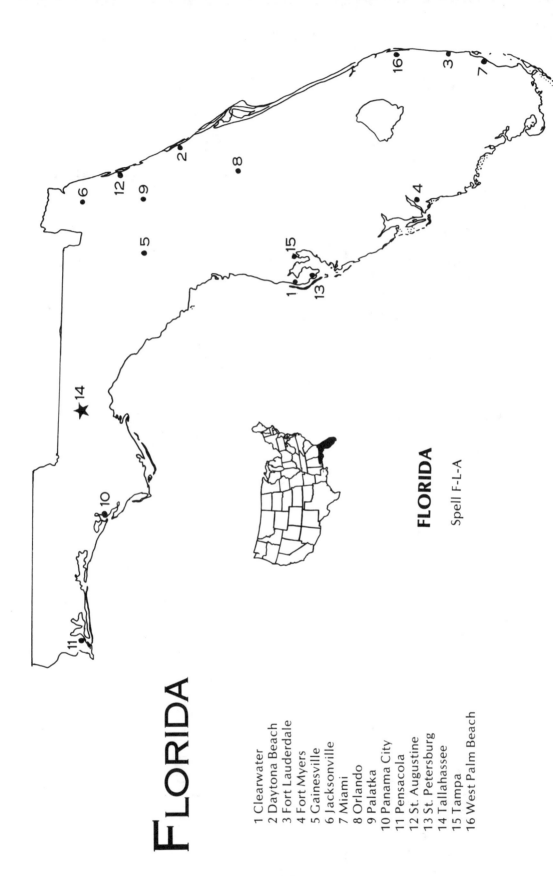

FLORIDA

1 Clearwater
2 Daytona Beach
3 Fort Lauderdale
4 Fort Myers
5 Gainesville
6 Jacksonville
7 Miami
8 Orlando
9 Palatka
10 Panama City
11 Pensacola
12 St. Augustine
13 St. Petersburg
14 Tallahassee
15 Tampa
16 West Palm Beach

FLORIDA

Spell F-L-A

‡1a **CLEARWATER**

Spell C-W

3a **FORT LAUDERDALE**

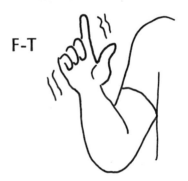

F-T

Spell F-T; L circles

‡1b **CLEARWATER**

Flat O's in front of
chest open to 5's; then W
touches chin

3b **FORT LAUDERDALE**

F-T

Spell F-T; shake L

4 **FORT MYERS**

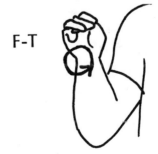

F-T

Spell F-T; M circles

‡2 **DAYTONA BEACH**

Spell D-B

5   GAINESVILLE

G taps on back of S-hand, fingers up

‡6b   JACKSONVILLE

Shake J

‡6a   JACKSONVILLE

J brushes on top of S

6c   JACKSONVILLE

Spell J-A-X

9a PALATKA

P circles on cheek

7 MIAMI

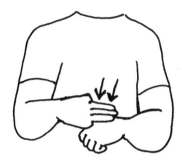

M, 3rd finger, taps on
back of S-hand

9b PALATKA

P twists on cheek

‡8 ORLANDO

Shake O

9c PALATKA

P taps on cheek

‡10 PANAMA CITY

Spell P-C

12a ST. AUGUSTINE

S-T

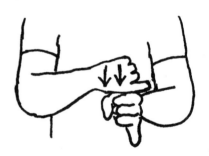

Spell S-T, A circles

‡11a PENSACOLA

Middle finger of P taps palm

‡12b ST. AUGUSTINE

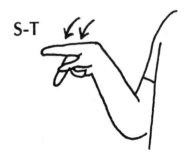

Side of right I taps on index - side of left I

11b PENSACOLA

Index finger of P taps palm

13a ST. PETERSBURG

S-T

Spell S-T, P nods

13b ST. PETERSBURG

S touches fingertips
and P touches heel of
flat palm

14b TALLAHASSEE

T circles, then touches
temple

13c ST. PETERSBURG

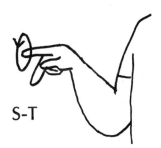

S-T

Spell S-T, P circles

15 TAMPA

T taps palm

‡14a TALLAHASSEE ★

Index circles near
temple, then touches
temple

16 WEST PALM BEACH

Spell W-P-B

GEORGIA

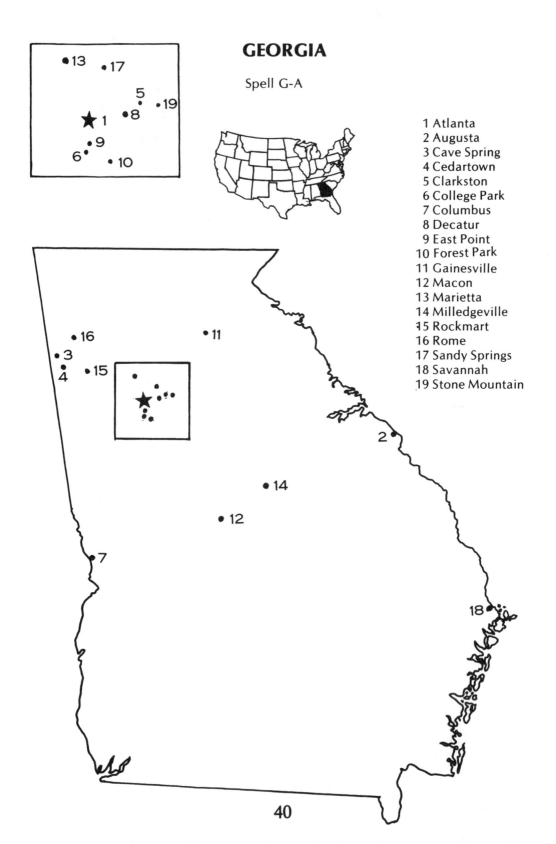

GEORGIA

Spell G-A

1 Atlanta
2 Augusta
3 Cave Spring
4 Cedartown
5 Clarkston
6 College Park
7 Columbus
8 Decatur
9 East Point
10 Forest Park
11 Gainesville
12 Macon
13 Marietta
14 Milledgeville
15 Rockmart
16 Rome
17 Sandy Springs
18 Savannah
19 Stone Mountain

Georgia

1 ATLANTA ★

A taps side of chest,
arcs to tap other side

‡2a AUGUSTA

Shake A

2b AUGUSTA

A wiggles down

3a CAVE SPRING

Spell C-S

3b CAVE SPRING

C closes to S on top
of S-hand

4 CEDARTOWN

Thumb of C taps side
of chest, arcs to tap
other side

41

5 CLARKSTON

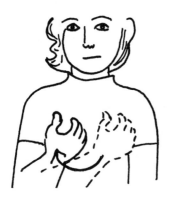

Thumb of C taps side
of chest, arcs to tap
other side

6 COLLEGE PARK

Spell C-P

7 COLUMBUS

8 DECATUR

D taps side of chest,
arcs to tap other side

9 EAST POINT

Spell E-P

10 FOREST PARK

Spell F-P

Shake C

11 GAINESVILLE

G circles

14a MILLEDGEVILLE

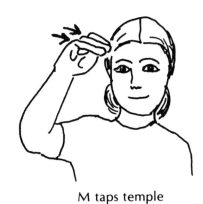

M taps temple

12 MACON

M fingers touch left
shoulder, then right

14b MILLEDGEVILLE

5 -hand swings sideways
from wrist, fingers
pointing at eyes

13 MARIETTA

M taps side of chest,
arcs to tap other side

15 ROCKMART

R twists at chin several
times

16a **ROME**

Shake R

‡18a **SAVANNAH**

S taps side of chest,
arcs to tap other side

16b **ROME**

R taps side of chest,
arcs to tap other side

‡18b **SAVANNAH**

S circles

‡17 **SANDY SPRINGS**

Open and close S as hand moves
to side

19 **STONE MOUNTAIN**

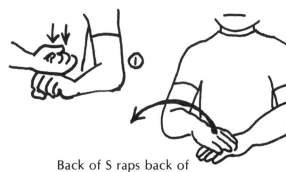

Back of S raps back of
S twice; right hand
traces smooth mountain
top

NOTES

HAWAII

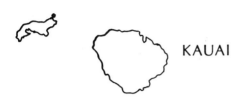

KAUAI

Pearl City
Pearl Harbor
Honolulu
Waikiki
Diamond Head

HAWAII

H circles in front of
face

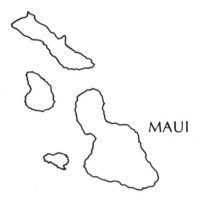

MAUI

HAWAII

"Big Island"

46

Hawaii

H-hand circles face;

Kauai

K-hand circles face

BIG ISLAND

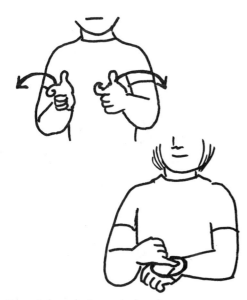

Bent I-hands face each other, arc apart,

Side of I circles on back of left S

Maui

M-hand circles face

‡1 **DIAMOND HEAD**

D taps temple

‡2 **HONOLULU** ★

H nods, arcs to right, nods again

3 **PEARL CITY**

Spell P-C

4 **PEARL HARBOR**

Spell P-H

5 **WAIKIKI**

Shake W

NOTES

IDAHO

IDAHO

Spell I-D-A-H-O

1 American Falls
2 Blackfoot
3 Boise
4 Coeur d' Alene
5 Fairfield
6 Glenns Ferry
7 Grand View
8 Idaho Falls
9 Kings Hill
10 Lava Hot Springs
11 Lewiston
12 Mountain Home
13 New Plymouth
14 Pocatello
15 Post Falls
16 Richfield
17 Sandpoint
18 Shoshone
19 Sugar City
20 Sun Valley
21 Twin Falls
22 White Bird
23 Yellowpine

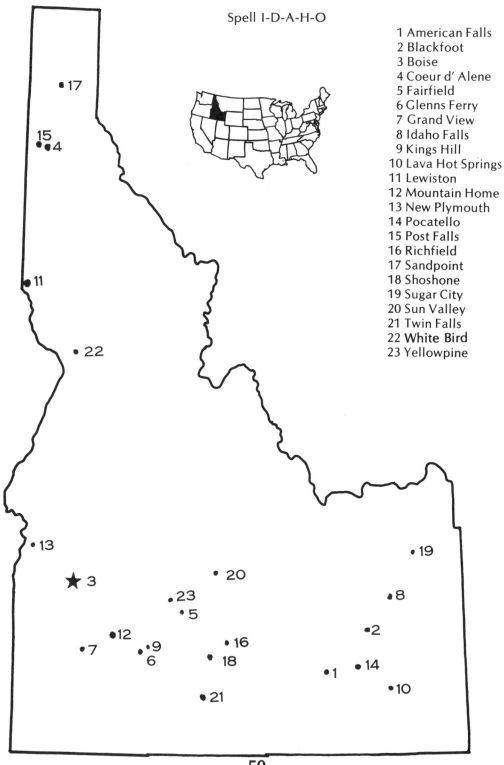

50

1 AMERICAN FALLS

F-A-L-L-S

5 hands interlock, circle
together; spell F-A-L-L-S

2 BLACKFOOT

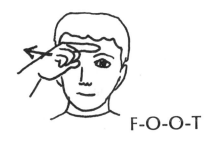

F-O-O-T

Index finger slides across
brow; spell F-O-O-T

‡3 BOISE ★

Shake B

4 COEUR D'ALENE

Spell C-D-A

‡5 FAIRFIELD

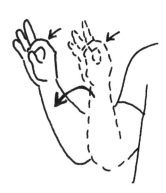

Nod F, arc to right,
nod again

‡6 GLENNS FERRY

Spell G-F

7 GRAND VIEW

Spell G-V

‡8 IDAHO FALLS

Spell I-F

9   KINGS HILL

H-I-L-L

K touches left shoulder,
then right hip; spell
H-I-L-L

‡11a LEWISTON

Shake L

11b   LEWISTON

L on nose; close to
hold nose

10   LAVA HOT SPRINGS

L-A-V-A

Spell L-A-V-A; claw hand
moves out from open
mouth; flat O opens to S,
up through palm-
right C

12   MOUNTAIN HOME

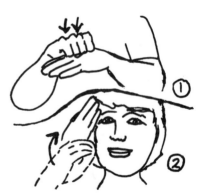

S taps on back of palm
down hand; flat O at side
of mouth opens to B
on cheek

‡13 NEW PLYMOUTH

Spell N-P

‡18 SHOSHONE

14 POCATELLO

Open and close 5 as
hand moves to side

F moves out from cheek
in short hops

19 SUGAR CITY

15 POST FALLS

Spell P-F

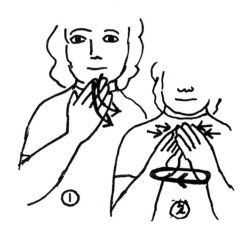

‡16 RICHFIELD

Spell R-F

Brush fingertips
downward off chin; tap
tip of flat-hands twice,
both circling

‡17 SANDPOINT

Spell S-P

20 SUN VALLEY

Spell S-V

‡23 YELLOWPINE

‡21 TWIN FALLS

Spell T-F

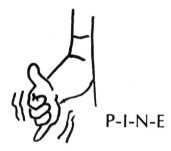

P-I-N-E

‡22 WHITE BIRD

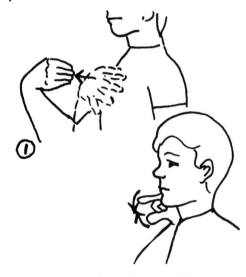

Shake Y at wrist, spell
P-I-N-E

5 touches chest and
moves forward to flat O;
G at mouth closes
several times

NOTES

ILLINOIS

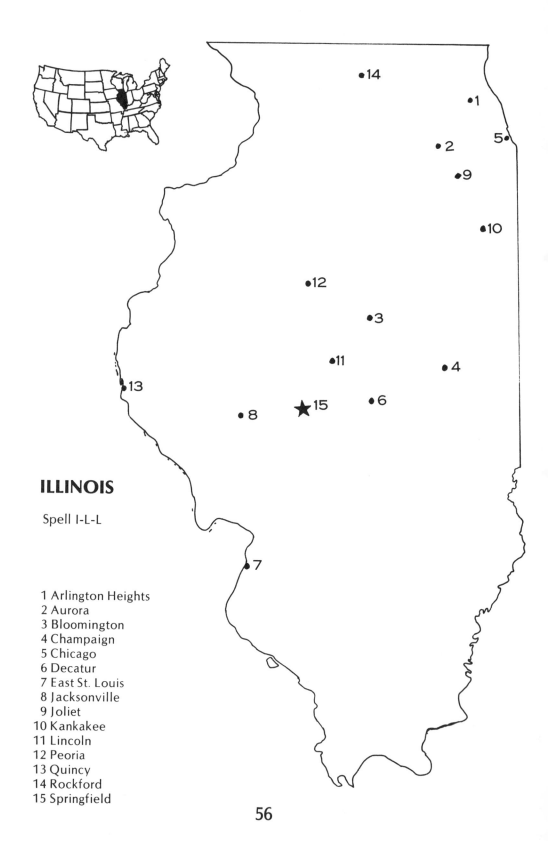

ILLINOIS

Spell I-L-L

1 Arlington Heights
2 Aurora
3 Bloomington
4 Champaign
5 Chicago
6 Decatur
7 East St. Louis
8 Jacksonville
9 Joliet
10 Kankakee
11 Lincoln
12 Peoria
13 Quincy
14 Rockford
15 Springfield

1   **ARLINGTON HEIGHTS**

Spell A-H

2a   **AURORA**

Flat palm in; A circles
near palm

‡2b   **AURORA**

Shake A

‡3a   **BLOOMINGTON**

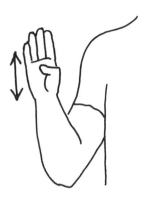

B bobs

‡3b   **BLOOMINGTON**

B circles

4   **CHAMPAIGN**

Spell C-H several times

57

‡5 **CHICAGO**

C traces a 7

‡8a **JACKSONVILLE**

J sweeps top of A

‡6 **DECATUR**

Shake D

8b **JACKSONVILLE**

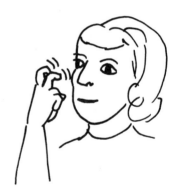

Palm-in V, in front of face; bend fingers several times

7 **EAST ST. LOUIS**

Spell E-S-T-L

‡9a **JOLIET**

Spell J

‡9b JOLIET

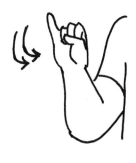

Shake J

12a PEORIA

P rotates in mid-air

10 KANKAKEE

Nod K, arc to right,
repeat twice

‡12b PEORIA

Shake P

11 LINCOLN

L touches shoulder, then
moves straight ahead

‡13 QUINCY

Q circles

15 SPRINGFIELD ★

G touches palm-out B
and sweeps downward
twice

14 ROCKFORD

R bobs

NOTES

Michigan City •

South Bend •

Fort Wayne •

Lafayette •

Anderson •
• Noblesville

Richmond •

★ Indianapolis

• Greencastle

• Terre Haute

• Columbus
• Bloomington

• Washington

• Evansville

INDIANA

62

INDIANA

Spell I-N-D

‡1 ANDERSON

Shake A

‡4 EVANSVILLE

Shake E

‡·2 BLOOMINGTON

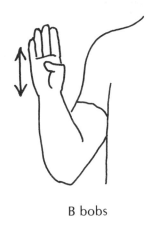

B bobs

5 FORT WAYNE

Spell F-W

6 GREENCASTLE

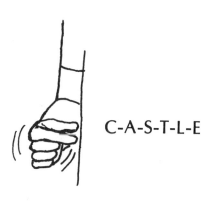

C-A-S-T-L-E

3 COLUMBUS

Thumb of C taps center
of forehead

63

Shake G, spell C-A-S-T-L-E

‡7   **INDIANAPOLIS** ★

I traces a 7

‡8   **LAFAYETTE**

Spell L-A-F

9   **MICHIGAN CITY**

Spell M-I-C-H C-I-T-Y

‡10   **NOBLESVILLE**

Shake N

‡11a **RICHMOND**

R traces a 7

‡11b **RICHMOND**

Shake R

‡12 **SOUTH BEND**

Spell S-B

‡14 **WASHINGTON**

Palm-in W from shoulder
circles forward and right

13 **TERRE HAUTE**

Spell T-H

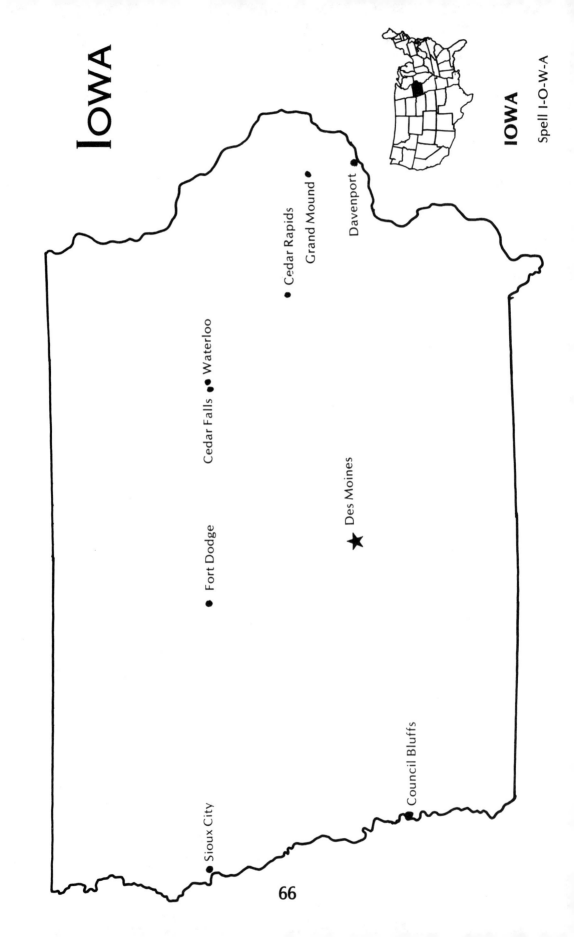

IOWA

IOWA

Spell I-O-W-A

Cedar Rapids

Grand Mound

Davenport

Waterloo

Cedar Falls

Des Moines

Fort Dodge

Council Bluffs

Sioux City

66

‡1 **CEDAR FALLS**

Spell C-F

6 **FORT DODGE**

Spell F-D

2 **CEDAR RAPIDS**

Spell C-R

‡7 **GRAND MOUND**

Spell G-M

‡3 **COUNCIL BLUFFS**

Spell C-B

‡8 **SIOUX CITY**

Spell S-C

4 **DAVENPORT**

Spell D-A-V

9 **WATERLOO**

L-O-O

5 **DES MOINES** ★

Spell D-M

W touches chin; spell
L-O-O

KANSAS

KANSAS

Spell K-A-N

Leavenworth•

Kansas City•
Overland Park•

Olathe•

Topeka ★

Emporia•

Junction City•

Wichita•

Pittsburg•

‡1　**EMPORIA**

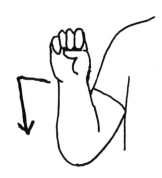

E traces a 7

‡2　**JUNCTION CITY**

Spell J-C

‡3　**KANSAS CITY**

Spell K-C

4　**LEAVENWORTH**

Spell L-W

‡5　**OLATHE**

O traces a 7

6　**OVERLAND PARK**

Spell O-P

‡7 **PITTSBURG**

F moves down side
of chest, repeat

‡9 **WICHITA**

W traces a 7

‡8 **TOPEKA** ★

T traces a 7

NOTES

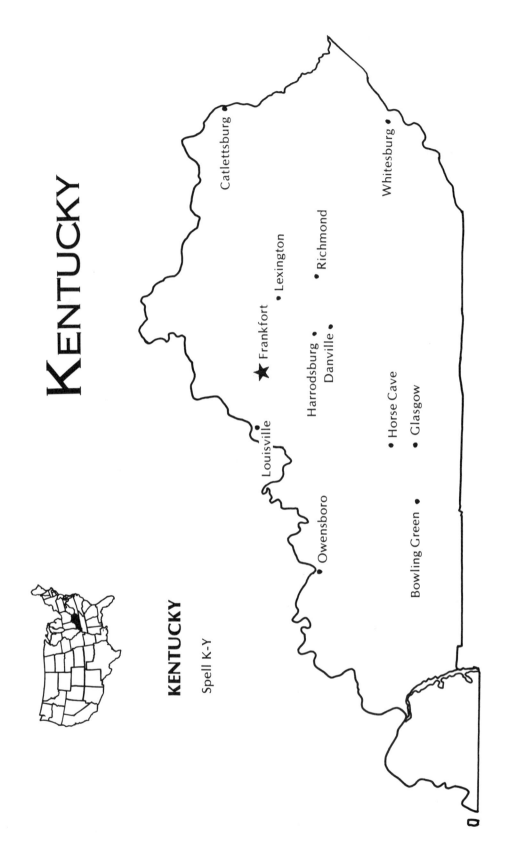

KENTUCKY

KENTUCKY

Spell K-Y

Catlettsburg

Whitesburg

Lexington

Richmond

Frankfort

Harrodsburg
Danville

Louisville

Horse Cave

Glasgow

Owensboro

Bowling Green

1a BOWLING GREEN

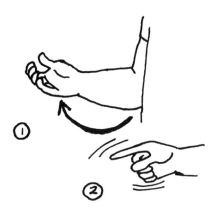

Claw-hand, palm-up, arcs slightly upward; shake G

1b BOWLING GREEN

Spell B-G

2a CATLETTSBURG

Spell C-A-T

2b CATLETTSBURG

Claw-hand scratches cheek

‡3 DANVILLE

Shake D

‡4 FRANKFORT ★

F touches fingertips, then heel of flat hand

‡5 GLASGOW

Shake G

‡6 HARRODSBURG

Nod H, arc to right, nod again

7 HORSE CAVE

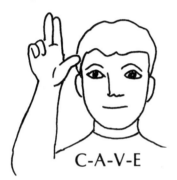

C-A-V-E

Thumb on temple, flat H-finger; spell C-A-V-E

8 LEXINGTON

Spell L-E-X

9 LOUISVILLE

Shake L

‡10 OWENSBORO

Shake O

‡11 RICHMOND

R traces a 7

‡12 WHITESBURG

5 on chest moves outward, closing to a flat-O

NOTES

LOUISIANA

LOUISIANA

Spell L-A

1 Alexandria
2 Baton Rouge
3 Denham Springs
4 Hammond
5 Lafayette
6 Lake Arthur
7 Lake Charles
8 Monroe
9 New Orleans
10 Opelousas
11 Shreveport
12 Ville Platte

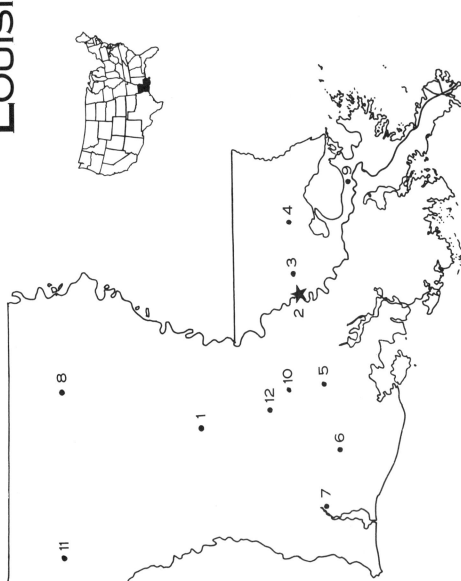

‡1 **ALEXANDRIA**

Spell A-L-E-X

7 **LAKE CHARLES**

Spell L-C

2 **BATON ROUGE** ★

Spell B-R

8 **MONROE**

Spell M-O-N

‡3 **DENHAM SPRINGS**

Spell D-S

9a **NEW ORLEANS**

O brushes off heel
of hand, repeat;

‡4 **HAMMOND**

Spell H-A-M

‡5 **LAFAYETTE**

Spell L-A-F

9b **NEW ORLEANS**

6 **LAKE ARTHUR**

Spell L-A

F brushes off heel of hand, repeat

‡10a **OPELOUSAS**

Nod O, arc to right,
nod again

‡11 **SHREVEPORT**

Spell S on fingertips
and P on heel of palm

‡10b **OPELOUSAS**

O traces a 7

‡12 **VILLE PLATTE**

Spell V-P

NOTES

Maine

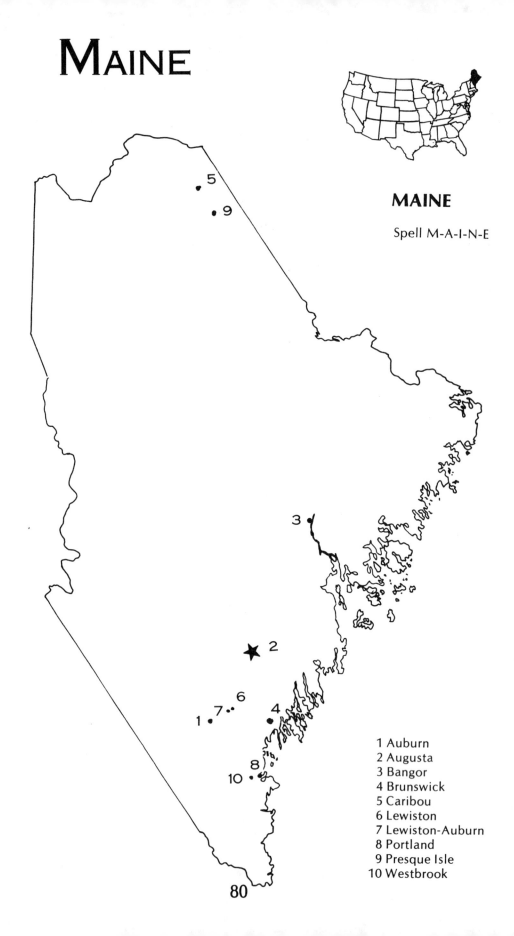

MAINE

Spell M-A-I-N-E

5

9

3

2

6

7 4

1

8

10

80

1 Auburn
2 Augusta
3 Bangor
4 Brunswick
5 Caribou
6 Lewiston
7 Lewiston-Auburn
8 Portland
9 Presque Isle
10 Westbrook

Maine

‡1 AUBURN

Spell A

‡2 AUGUSTA ★

Index finger circles
at temple and touches
temple

3 BANGOR

Index finger twists
into side of neck

4 BRUNSWICK

S-hands cross at wrists,
open to 5's

‡5 CARIBOU

Poke clawhands on
puffy cheeks

‡6 LEWISTON

Spell L

81

‡7 **LEWISTON-AUBURN**
Spell L-A

9 **PRESQUE ISLE**

Spell P-I

8a **PORTLAND**

P-middle finger bounces
on palm

‡10 **WESTBROOK**

Index finger twists
into chin

‡8b **PORTLAND**

P nods

NOTES

MARYLAND

MARYLAND

Spell M-D

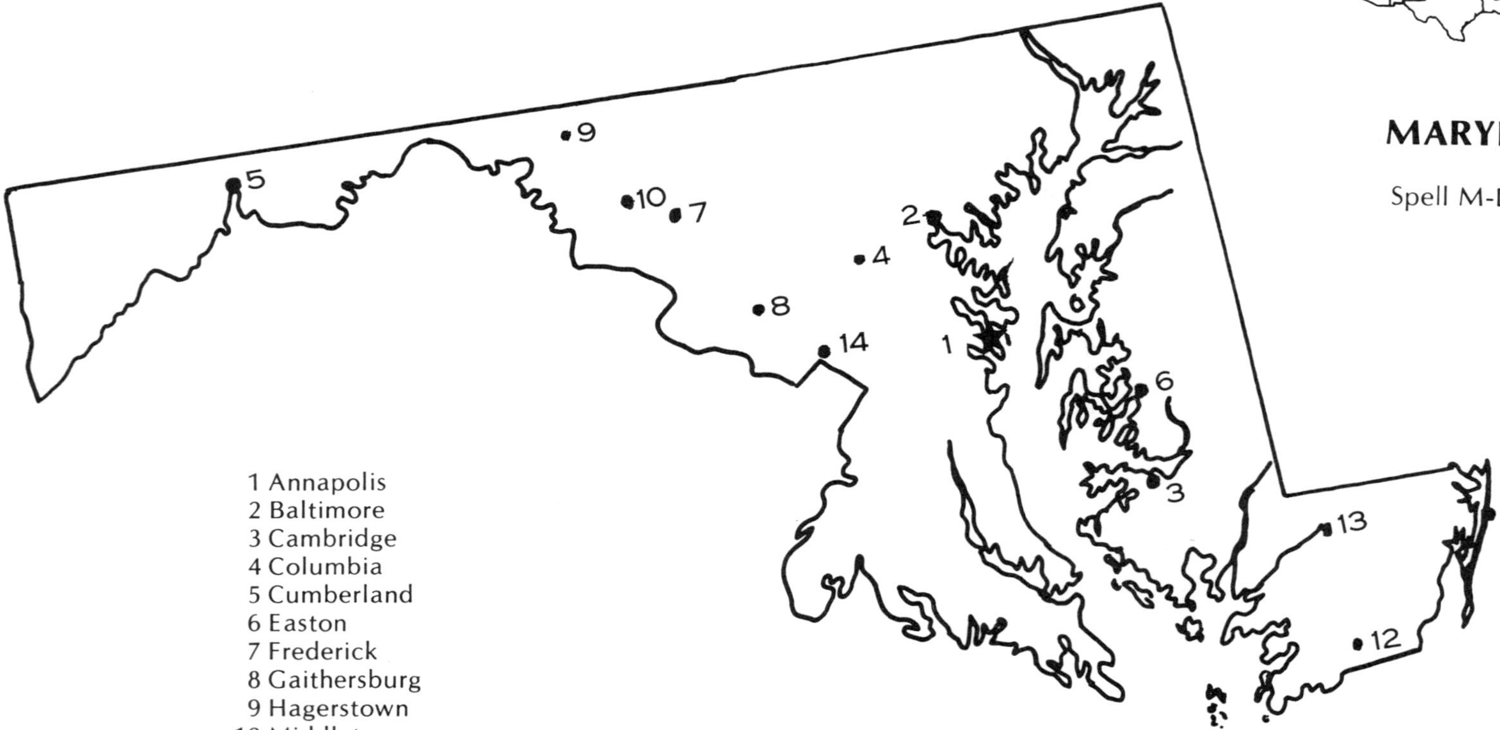

1 Annapolis
2 Baltimore
3 Cambridge
4 Columbia
5 Cumberland
6 Easton
7 Frederick
8 Gaithersburg
9 Hagerstown
10 Middletown
11 Ocean City
12 Pocomoke City
13 Salisbury
14 Silver Spring

‡1 **ANNAPOLIS** ★

Shake A

‡4 **COLUMBIA**

Shake C

2 **BALTIMORE**

B nods

5 **CUMBERLAND**

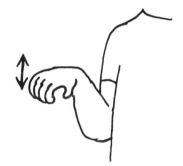

C, palm down, bobs

3 **CAMBRIDGE**

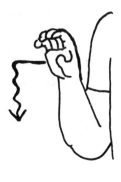

C moves to side,
then wiggles down

‡6 **EASTON**

Shake E

‡7   FREDERICK

Shake F

‡9   HAGERSTOWN

Nod H, arc to right,
nod again

‡8   GAITHERSBURG

G circles

10   MIDDLETOWN

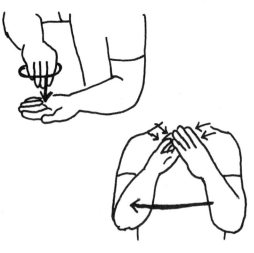

Bent hand circles
and touches palm; then
B fingertips touch,
moving to side

‡11 OCEAN CITY

Spell O-C

‡12 POCOMOKE CITY

Spell P-C

‡13a SALISBURY

S wiggles down

‡14 SILVER SPRING

Open and close S as hand moves to side

13b SALISBURY

S hits left B and moves up

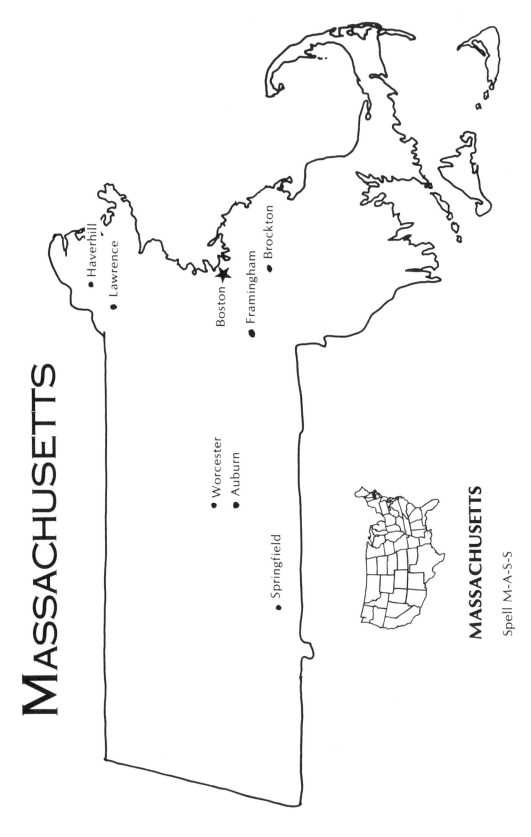

MASSACHUSETTS

Haverhill
Lawrence
Boston
Framingham
Brockton
Worcester
Auburn
Springfield

MASSACHUSETTS

Spell M-A-S-S

1 AUBURN

A-U

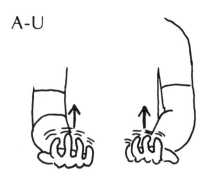

Spell A-U; palm-up
bent 5's move upward,
fluttering fingers

‡2 BOSTON ★

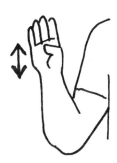

B bobs

‡3 BROCKTON

Shake B

‡4 FRAMINGHAM

Shake F

‡5 HAVERHILL

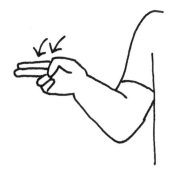

H nods

89

6a **LAWRENCE**

L bobs

‡7a **SPRINGFIELD**

S traces a 7

7b **SPRINGFIELD**

Palm-in flat O
grows through left C,
to a palm-in 5;
spell F

‡6b **LAWRENCE**

L shakes

‡8 **WORCESTER**

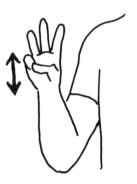

W bobs

NOTES

MICHIGAN

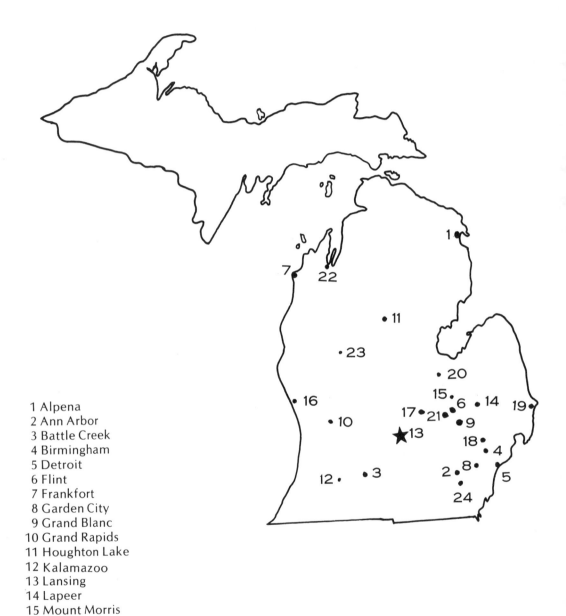

1 Alpena
2 Ann Arbor
3 Battle Creek
4 Birmingham
5 Detroit
6 Flint
7 Frankfort
8 Garden City
9 Grand Blanc
10 Grand Rapids
11 Houghton Lake
12 Kalamazoo
13 Lansing
14 Lapeer
15 Mount Morris
16 Muskegon
17 Owosso
18 Pontiac
19 Port Huron
20 Saginaw
21 Swartz Creek
22 Traverse City
23 Woodland Park
24 Ypsilanti

MICHIGAN

Spell M-I-C-H

MICHIGAN

Outline 5-hand with index of other hand, the following is used to set the entire state and then the person will point to the place on one hand or the other to indicate the city by its location

MICHIGAN

a.   b.   c.

Place flat hands in the position of upper & lower peninsulas of Michigan. The upper peninsula may vary.

Michigan

‡1 **ALPENA**

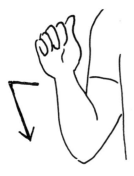

A traces a 7

5 **DETROIT**

D traces a 7

‡2 **ANN ARBOR**

Nod A, arc to right,
nod again

‡6 **FLINT**

F traces a 7

‡3 **BATTLE CREEK**

Spell B-C

‡7 **FRANKFORT**

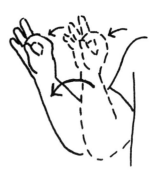

Nod F, arc to right,
nod again

‡4 **BIRMINGHAM**

B traces a 7

8 **GARDEN CITY**

Spell G-C

94

‡9 GRAND BLANC

Spell G-B

‡10 GRAND RAPIDS

Spell G-R

11 HOUGHTON LAKE

Spell H-L

12 KALAMAZOO

K traces a 7

13 LANSING ★

L circles at temple
and touches temple

14 LAPEER

L traces a 7

15 MOUNT MORRIS

Nod M, arc to right,
nod again

‡16 MUSKEGON

M traces a 7

‡17 OWOSSO

O traces a 7

‡18 PONTIAC

F touches near nose,
then temple

19 PORT HURON

Spell P-H

20 SAGINAW

Spell S-A-G

‡21 SWARTZ CREEK

Spell S-C

‡22 TRAVERSE CITY

Spell T-C

‡23 WOODLAND PARK

Spell W-P

24 YPSILANTI

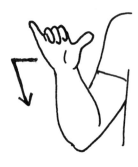

Y traces a 7

NOTES

Minnesota

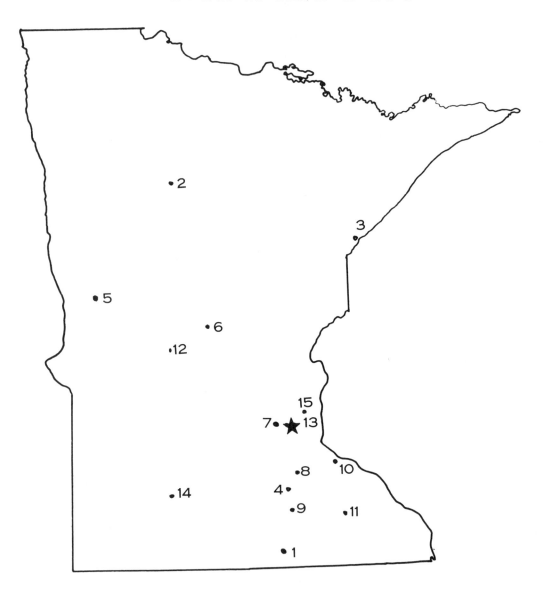

MINNESOTA

Spell M-I-N-N

98

1 Albert Lea
2 Bemidji
3 Duluth
4 Fairbault
5 Fergus Falls
6 Little Falls
7 Minneapolis
8 Northfield
9 Owatonna
10 Red Wing
11 Rochester
12 Sauk Centre
13 St. Paul
14 **Springfield**
15 White Bear Lake

1 ALBERT LEA

Spell A-L

2 BEMIDJI

B's touch, palm out;
arc to sides; make J's

3 DULUTH

D moves out and up
from index on mid-
forehead

‡4 FAIRBAULT

F nods

‡5 FERGUS FALLS

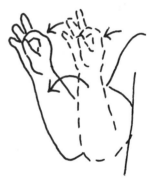

Nod F, arc to right,
nod again

‡6 LITTLE FALLS

Spell L-F

99

7   **MINNEAPOLIS**

D-fingertips tap heart

‡10   **RED WING**

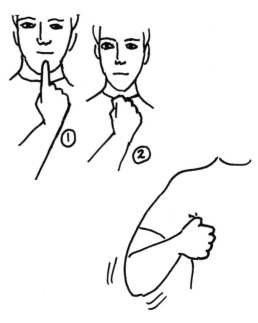

Palm-in, index finger
touches chin, brushes
down and closes;
B-hand touches
shoulder and flaps
a little

‡8   **NORTHFIELD**

Spell N-F

‡9   **OWATONNA**

O bobs

‡11   **ROCHESTER**

R nods

‡12 ST. PAUL ★

S circles at temple;
P touches temple

‡15 WHITE BEAR LAKE

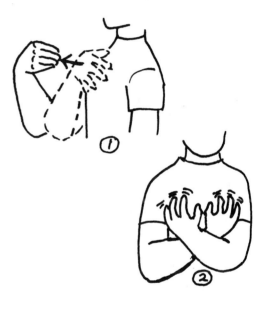

5 on chest moves out-
ward, closing to a flat-O;
Cross wrists and scratch
chest

‡13 SAUK CENTRE

Spell S-C

‡14 SPRINGFIELD

Spell S-F

MISSISSIPPI

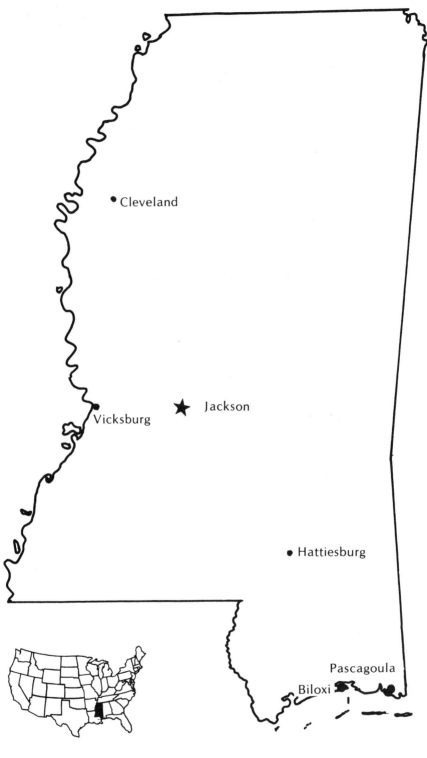

- •Cleveland

★ Jackson

•Vicksburg

•Hattiesburg

Pascagoula

Biloxi

MISSISSIPPI

Spell M-I-S-S

Mississippi

‡1 **BILOXI**

Shake B

‡2 **CLEVELAND**

C wiggles down

‡3 **HATTIESBURG**

Spell H-B

‡4 **JACKSON** ★

Shake J

5 **PASCAGOULA**

Spell P-A-S-C

‡6a **VICKSBURG**

Shake V

6b **VICKSBURG**

V wiggles down

MISSOURI

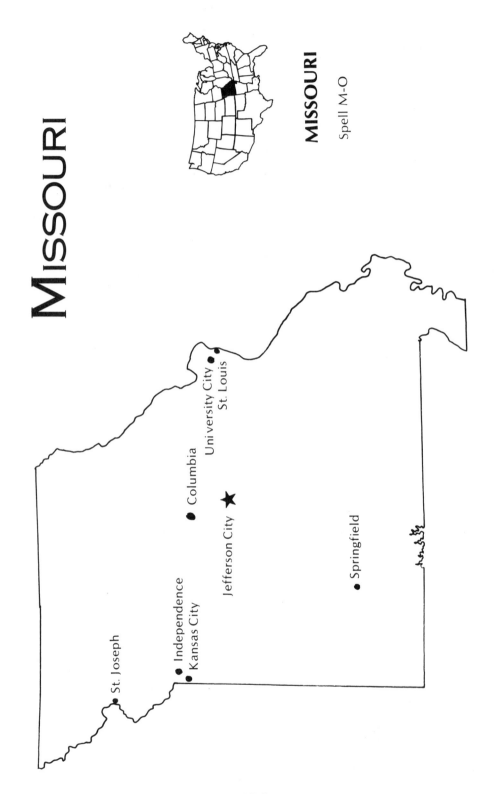

MISSOURI

Spell M-O

St. Joseph

Independence
Kansas City

Columbia

University City
St. Louis

Jefferson City

Springfield

‡1 **COLUMBIA**

Shake C

‡2 **INDEPENDENCE**

I makes a 7

‡3 **JEFFERSON CITY** ★

Spell J-C

‡4 **KANSAS CITY**

Spell K-C

5 **ST. JOSEPH**

Spell S-T-J

6a **ST. LOUIS**

Spell S-T-L

6b **ST. LOUIS**

Spell S-L in an arc

7 **SPRINGFIELD**

Side of thumb and index of G touches fingertips of palm, then heel

8 **UNIVERSITY CITY**

Spell U-C

Montana

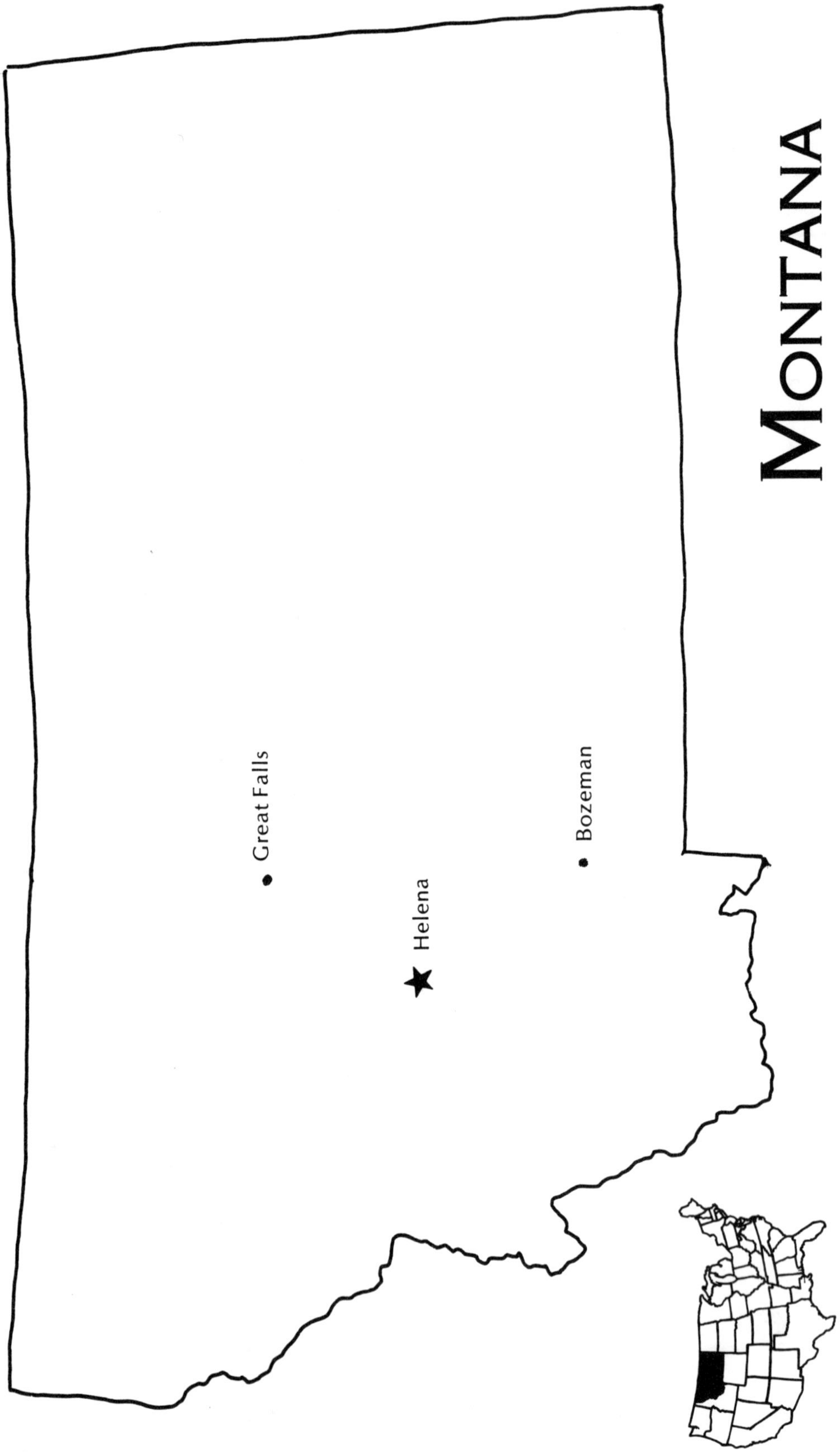

● Great Falls

Helena
★

● Bozeman

MONTANA

M hands separate to
side, move down, move
back to touch

HELENA

H circles forward

BOZEMAN

B makes a Z

GREAT FALLS

Spell G-F

NEBRASKA

NEBRASKA

Spell N-E-B

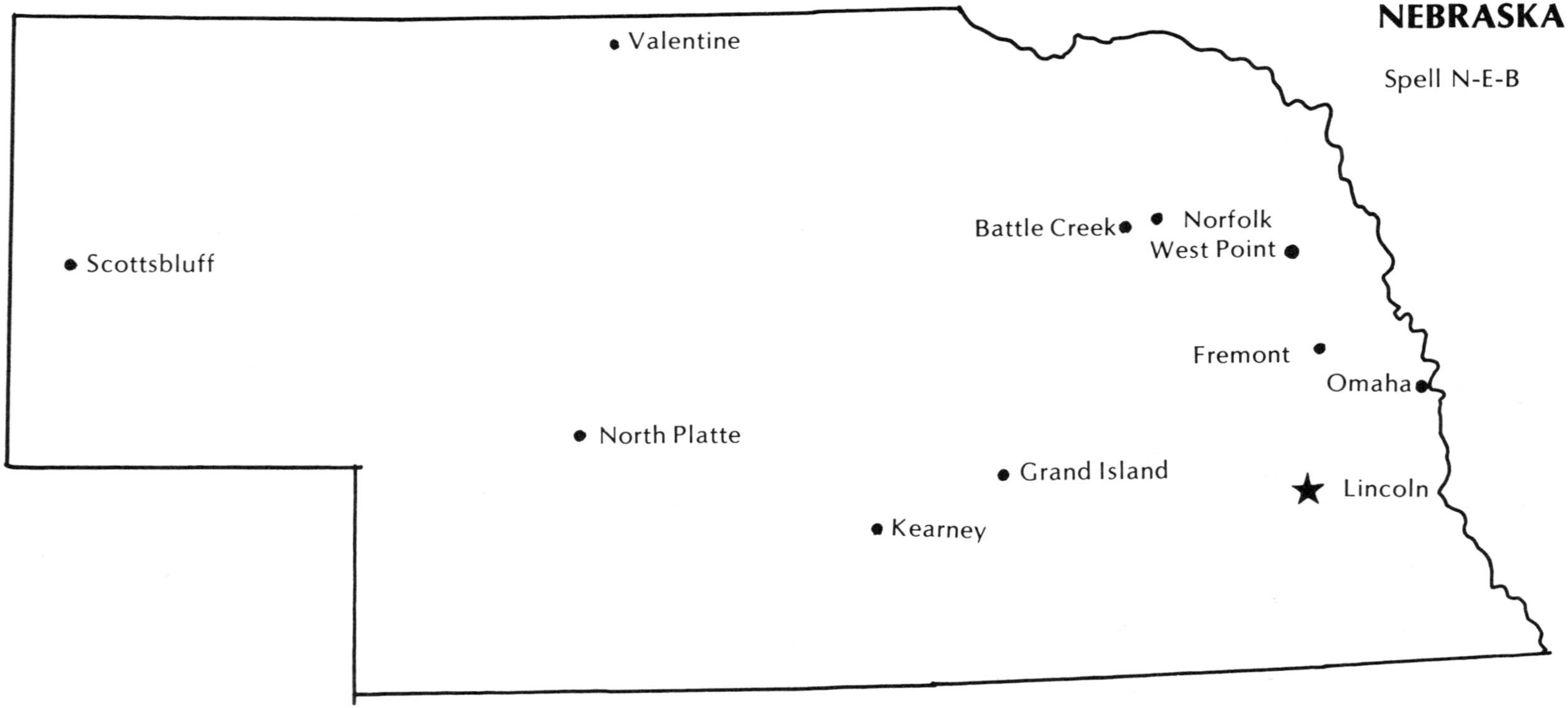

- Valentine
- Scottsbluff
- North Platte
- Battle Creek
- Norfolk
- West Point
- Fremont
- Omaha
- Grand Island
- Kearney
- ★ Lincoln

‡1   BATTLE CREEK

Spell B-C

‡2   FREMONT

Shake F

3   GRAND ISLAND

Spell G-I

‡4   KEARNEY

Shake K

‡5   LINCOLN

Shake L

‡6   NORFOLK

Shake N

‡7   NORTH PLATTE

Spell N-P

109

‡8a **OMAHA**

O circles

‡10 **VALENTINE**

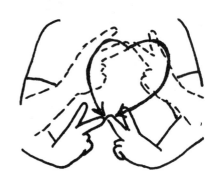

Outline heart with
V-fingers

‡8b **OMAHA**

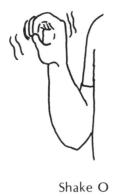

Shake O

‡11 **WEST POINT**

Spell W-P

‡9 **SCOTTSBLUFF**

Spell S-B

NOTES

● Reno

★

NEVADA

Las Vegas ●

NEVADA

Spell N-E-V

LAS VEGAS

Palm-out L pulls
down to V

RENO

Spell R-E-N-O

NEW HAMPSHIRE

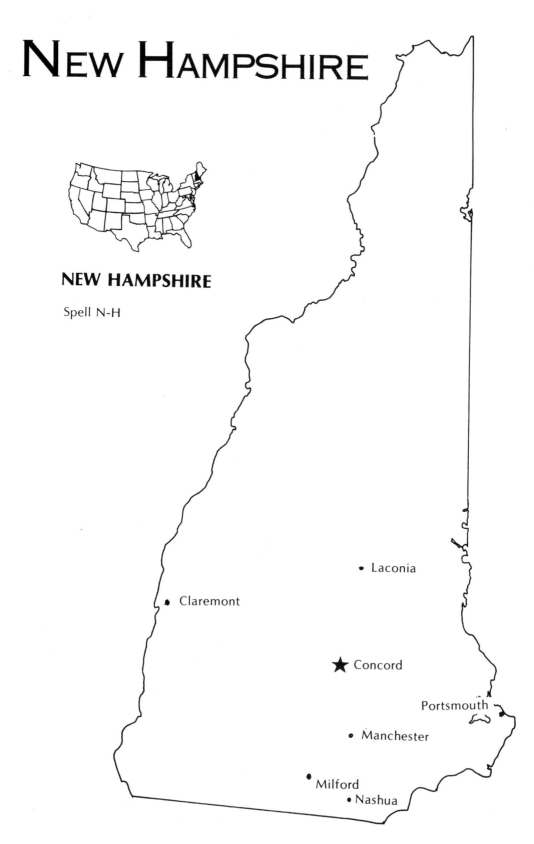

NEW HAMPSHIRE

Spell N-H

• Laconia

• Claremont

★ Concord

Portsmouth •

• Manchester

• Milford

• Nashua

‡1 **CLAREMONT**

C circles

3 **LACONIA**

L rises

‡2a **CONCORD** ★

C circles

4a **MANCHESTER**

M traces a 7

2b **CONCORD**

C circles at temple
and touches

‡4b **MANCHESTER**

M circles

115

‡5   MILFORD

Shake M

‡7a   PORTSMOUTH

P traces a 7

‡6   NASHUA

N circles

‡7b   PORTSMOUTH

Shake P

NOTES

NEW JERSEY

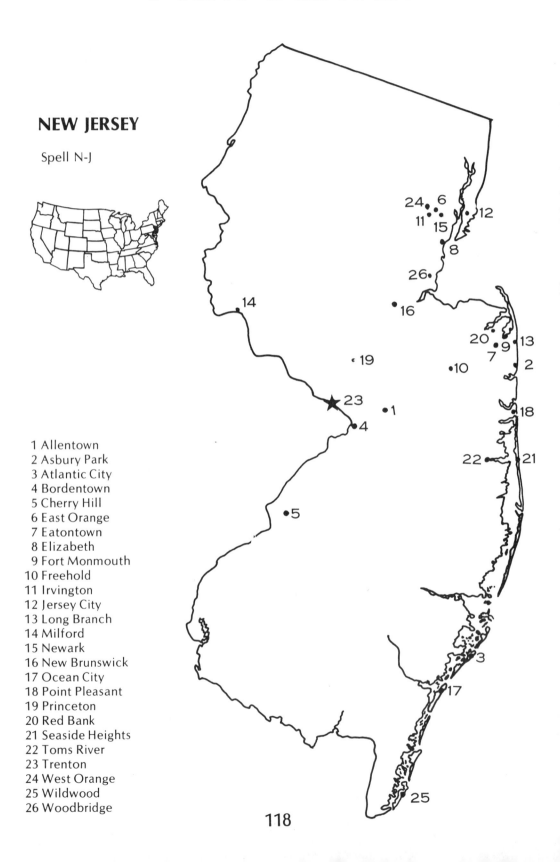

NEW JERSEY

Spell N-J

1 Allentown
2 Asbury Park
3 Atlantic City
4 Bordentown
5 Cherry Hill
6 East Orange
7 Eatontown
8 Elizabeth
9 Fort Monmouth
10 Freehold
11 Irvington
12 Jersey City
13 Long Branch
14 Milford
15 Newark
16 New Brunswick
17 Ocean City
18 Point Pleasant
19 Princeton
20 Red Bank
21 Seaside Heights
22 Toms River
23 Trenton
24 West Orange
25 Wildwood
26 Woodbridge

‡1 ALLENTOWN

A traces a 7

5 CHERRY HILL

H-I-L-L

Index of bent-V moves
along cheekbone twice;
spell H-I-L-L

‡2 ASBURY PARK

Spell A-P

‡3 ATLANTIC CITY

Spell A-C

6 EAST ORANGE

E moves to the right;
C at mouth closes to S
several times

4 BORDENTOWN

Shake B

119

7 EATONTOWN

Palm-in flat O nods
toward mouth; right palm
touches back of left hand;
fingertips touch at left,
separate, touch at right

10a FREEHOLD

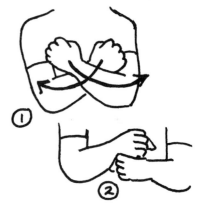

Fists, crossed at wrists,
separate and twist out;
right fist on top of
left fist

8 ELIZABETH

E, palm in at right
eye, shakes

10b FREEHOLD

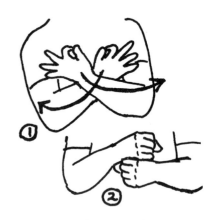

Palm-in F's, crossed
at wrists, separate and
twist to palm-out;
right fist on top of
left fist

9 FORT MONMOUTH

F-T

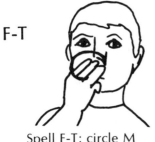

Spell F-T; circle M
at mouth

11a IRVINGTON

Palm-in I-hand at temple moves out in 2 arcs

11b **IRVINGTON**

I taps cheekbone

‡12 **JERSEY CITY**

Spell J-C

‡13 **LONG BRANCH**

Spell L-B

14 **MILFORD**

M-fingertips at corner of mouth slide back slightly

15 **NEWARK**

Spell N-E-W-K fluently

‡16 **NEW BRUNSWICK**

Spell N-B

‡17 **OCEAN CITY**

Spell O-C

18a POINT PLEASANT

Nod P, arc to right,
nod again

19 PRINCETON

P in palm, rises

18b POINT PLEASANT

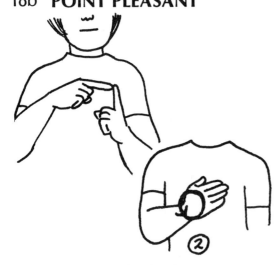

Horizontal index finger
approaches and touches
left vertical index
finger; palm rubs on
chest in circle

20 RED BANK

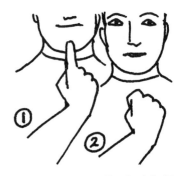

B-A-N-K

Palm-in, index finger
touches chin, brushes
down and closes;
spell B-A-N-K or B-K

‡21 SEASIDE HEIGHTS

Spell S-H

22 TOMS RIVER

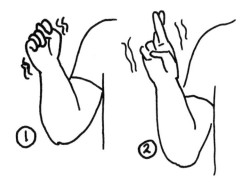

T, R shake

24 WEST ORANGE

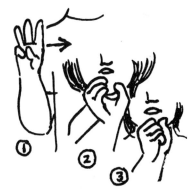

W moves to left;
C at mouth closes to S
several times

‡23a TRENTON ★

T traces a 7

‡25 WILDWOOD

Nod W, arc to right,
nod again

‡23b TRENTON

T taps one side of chest, arcs to tap
other side

26 WOODBRIDGE

Edge of right hand
saws on back of left
hand; fingertips of V
touch left palm, arc
to touch again near elbow

NEW MEXICO

NEW MEXICO

Spell N-M

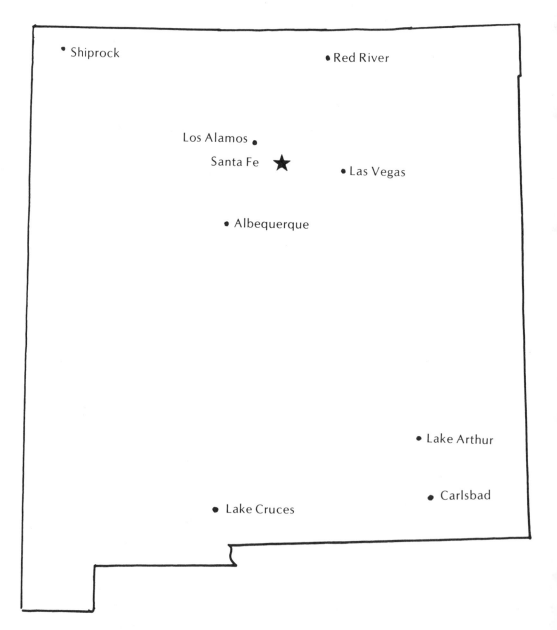

• Shiprock

• Red River

Los Alamos •

Santa Fe ★

• Las Vegas

• Albequerque

• Lake Arthur

• Carlsbad

• Lake Cruces

‡1 ALBUQUERQUE

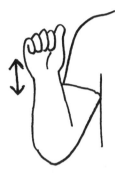

A bobs

3 LAKE ARTHUR

L taps temple; becomes
A on side of chin

2 CARLSBAD

C-L-S

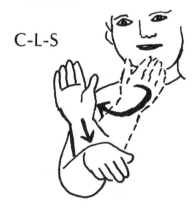

Spell C-L-S; palm-in
hand at mouth, twist
to palm-out and
throw down

4 LAS CRUCES

Spell L-C

5 LAS VEGAS

Spell L-V

‡6   LOS ALAMOS

Spell L-A

‡8a   SANTA FE

Spell S-F

‡8b   SANTA FE

7   RED RIVER

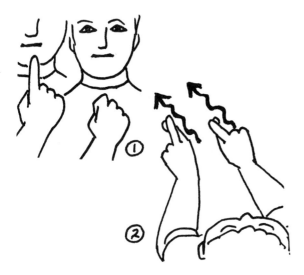

Palm-in, index finger
touches chin, brushes
down and closes;
palm-down R's ripple
forward to left up
and down

Fingertips of F
flutter up and down

9   SHIP ROCK

Side of 3 on flat
palm; both hands move
forward in slight
up-and-down motion

NOTES

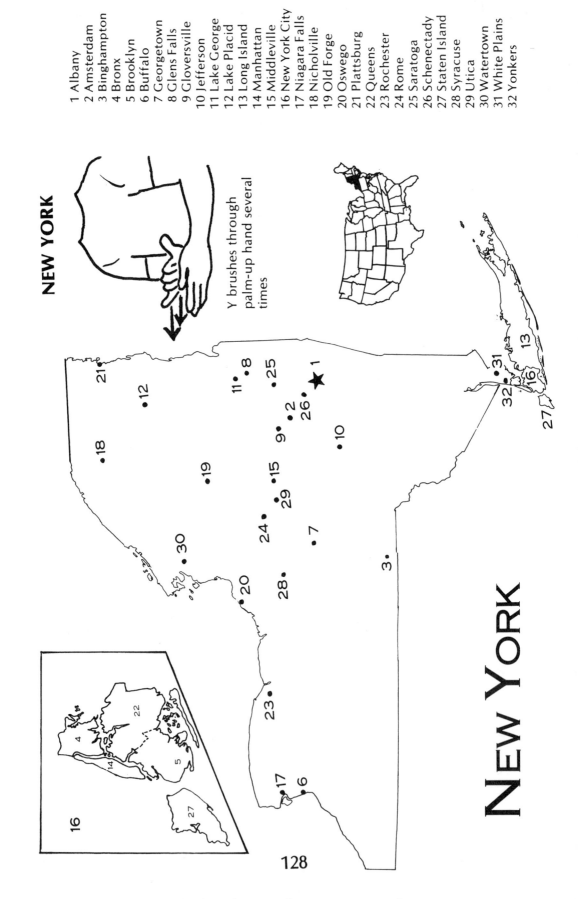

NEW YORK

Y brushes through
palm-up hand several
times

1 Albany
2 Amsterdam
3 Binghampton
4 Bronx
5 Brooklyn
6 Buffalo
7 Georgetown
8 Glens Falls
9 Cloversville
10 Jefferson
11 Lake George
12 Lake Placid
13 Long Island
14 Manhattan
15 Middleville
16 New York City
17 Niagara Falls
18 Nicholville
19 Old Forge
20 Oswego
21 Plattsburg
22 Queens
23 Rochester
24 Rome
25 Saratoga
26 Schenectady
27 Staten Island
28 Syracuse
29 Utica
30 Watertown
31 White Plains
32 Yonkers

NEW YORK

‡1 **ALBANY** ★

A traces a 7

‡2 **AMSTERDAM**

Shake A

‡3 **BINGHAMPTON**

B circles

4a **BRONX**

Spell B-X

4b **BRONX**

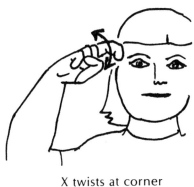

X twists at corner
of eye

‡5a **BROOKLYN**

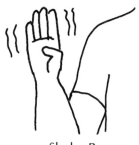

Shake B

‡5b **BROOKLYN**

B bobs

‡6a **BUFFALO**

B wiggles down

‡6b **BUFFALO**

Rock palm-in Y
on forehead

6c **BUFFALO**

Rock palm-in Y
on temple

‡7 **GEORGETOWN**

Spell G-T

‡8 **GLEN FALLS**

Spell G-F

‡9 **GLOVERSVILLE**

B, palm down; 5
scratches back of B

10 **JEFFERSON**

Spell J-J, moving to
the right

‡11 **LAKE GEORGE**

Spell L-G

12 **LAKE PLACID**

Spell L-P

‡13a LONG ISLAND

Index finger slides up
left arm; side of I
circles on back of
left S

14a MANHATTAN

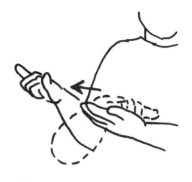

Quickly sweep palm
down Y off palm

14b MANHATTAN

Spell M-A-T-T

13b LONG ISLAND

ILY becomes I

15 MIDDLEVILLE

Bent hand circles
and touches palm;
then B-fingertips touch,
moving to side

13c LONG ISLAND

Spell L-I

16a NEW YORK CITY

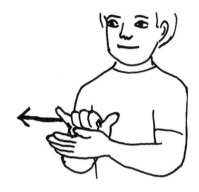

Palm-down Y slides
off left palm

16b NEW YORK CITY

C-I-T-Y

Palm-down Y slides
off left palm; spell
C-I-T-Y

‡17 NIAGARA FALLS

Spell N-F

‡18 NICHOLVILLE

Shake N

19 OLD FORGE

O on chin changes
to F

‡20 OSWEGO

O circles

132

‡21 PLATTSBURG

9 index and thumb brush down right shoulder rapidly several times

23b ROCHESTER

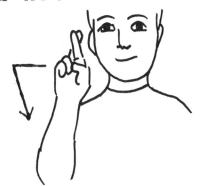

R starts at temple, then traces a 7

‡22 QUEENS

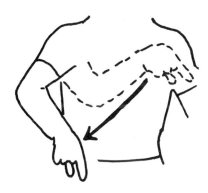

Q touches left shoulder, then right hip

‡24a ROME

Right X-finger brushes off tip of nose

‡23a ROCHESTER

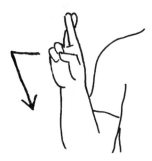

R traces a 7

‡24b ROME

G arcs down inward near nose

‡24c ROME

R touches mid-forehead
and nose

‡25 SARATOGA

A's, palms facing,
move alternately back
and forth, not touching

26 SCHENECTADY

Spell S-C-H

27 STATEN ISLAND

Spell S-I

28a SYRACUSE

Spell S-Y downwards

‡28b SYRACUSE

Spell S-Y

‡29 UTICA

U circles

30 WATERTOWN

Index finger of palm-
left W taps chin; finger-
tips touch at left,
separate; touch at right

‡31c **WHITE PLAINS**

Side of right I taps
on index-side of
left I

31a **WHITE PLAINS**

P-L-A-I-N-S

5 hand on chest moves
out to flat O; spell
P-L-A-I-N-S

‡31d **WHITE PLAINS**

Index and little fingers
out, right taps
left hand

‡31b **WHITE PLAINS**

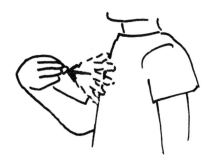

5 on chest moves out-
ward to a flat O

32 **YONKERS**

E-R

Palm-down Y slides
off left palm;
spell **E-R**

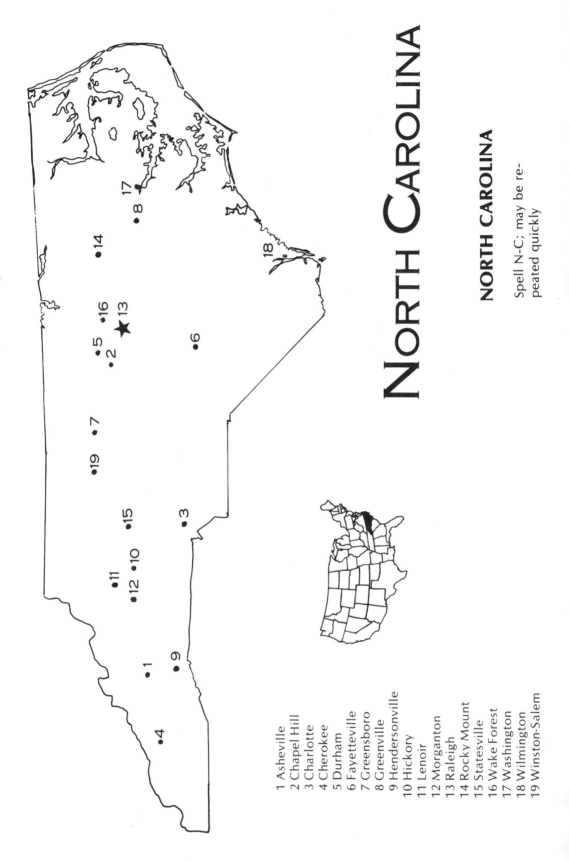

NORTH CAROLINA

NORTH CAROLINA

Spell N-C; may be re-
peated quickly

1 Asheville
2 Chapel Hill
3 Charlotte
4 Cherokee
5 Durham
6 Fayetteville
7 Greensboro
8 Greenville
9 Hendersonville
10 Hickory
11 Lenoir
12 Morganton
13 Raleigh
14 Rocky Mount
15 Statesville
16 Wake Forest
17 Washington
18 Wilmington
19 Winston-Salem

‡1 ASHEVILLE

Shake A

2 CHAPEL HILL

Spell C-H

‡3 CHARLOTTE

Shake C

‡4 CHEROKEE

F arcs back to ear

‡5a DURHAM

Shake D

5b DURHAM

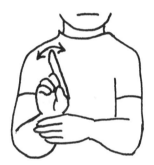

H eel of D-hand stays
on side of left;
index finger of D moves
side-to-side

‡6a FAYETTEVILLE

Nod F, arc to right,
nod again

‡6b **FAYETTEVILLE**

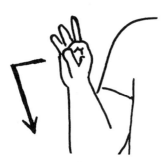

F traces a 7

‡6c **FAYETTEVILLE**

Heel of F-hand stays
of side of left;
fingers of F move
side-to-side

7a **GREENSBORO**

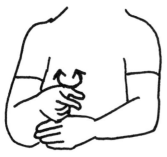

Heel of G-hand stays
on side of left, fingers
of G move side to
side

7b **GREENSBORO**

B-O-R-O

Shake G, spell **B-O-R-O**

7c **GREENSBORO**

G swings

‡7d **GREENSBORO**

Shake G

8 **GREENVILLE**

V-I-L-L-E

Shake G; spell **V-I-L-L-E**

9 HENDERSONVILLE

H circles

‡12b MORGANTON

M circles

10 HICKORY

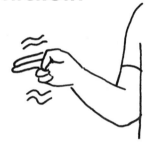

Shake H

‡13a RALEIGH ★

R traces a 7

‡11 LENOIR

Spell L-R

‡12a MORGANTON

Shake M

‡13b RALEIGH

Shake R

139

14 ROCKY MOUNT

Spell R-M

‡15 STATESVILLE

Shake S

16a WAKE FOREST

Spell W-F

16b WAKE FOREST

Spell U-S-1

‡17a WASHINGTON

W touches shoulder
and circles forward

17b WASHINGTON

W circles

18a WILMINGTON

W moves to side,
then wiggles down

18b WILMINGTON

W circles

19 WINSTON-SALEM

Spell W-S

NOTES

North Dakota

Grand Forks

Devils Lake

Bismarck

BISMARCK

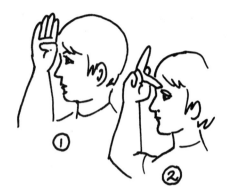

Spell B-K on forehead,
palm left

DEVIL'S LAKE

Spell D-L

GRAND FORKS

Spell G-F

OHIO

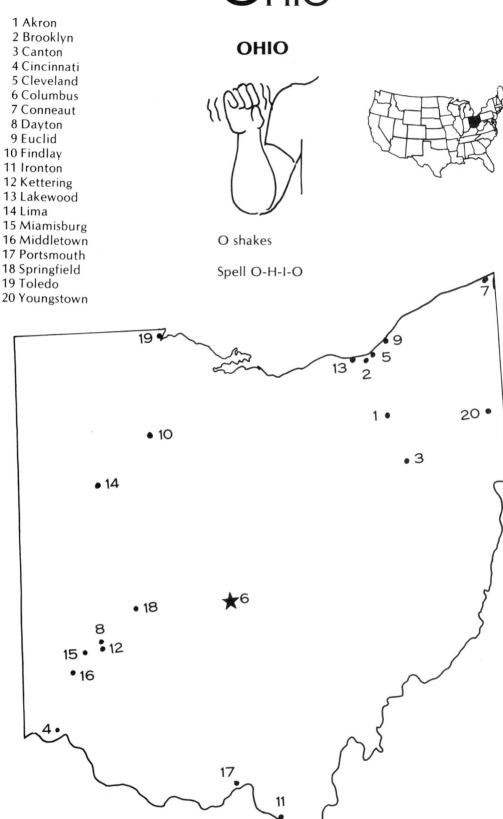

1 Akron
2 Brooklyn
3 Canton
4 Cincinnati
5 Cleveland
6 Columbus
7 Conneaut
8 Dayton
9 Euclid
10 Findlay
11 Ironton
12 Kettering
13 Lakewood
14 Lima
15 Miamisburg
16 Middletown
17 Portsmouth
18 Springfield
19 Toledo
20 Youngstown

OHIO

O shakes

Spell O-H-I-O

‡1 AKRON

X slides down cheek
several times

4 CINCINNATI

Spell C-I-N-N

5a CLEVELAND

Spell C-L-E-V

‡2 BROOKLYN

B bobs

‡5b CLEVELAND

C-thumb taps one side
of chest, then taps
other side

3 CANTON

C moves back over
shoulder several times

‡6a **COLUMBUS** ★

Shake C

6b **COLUMBUS**

Shake C at nose

‡7 **CONNEAUT**

Spell C-O-N-N

‡8 **DAYTON**

D bobs

‡9 **EUCLID**

Shake E

‡10 **FINDLAY**

Nod F, arc to right, nod again

‡11 **IRONTON**

Shake I

‡12 KETTERING

Shake K

15 MIAMISBURG

Shake M

13 LAKEWOOD

L taps one side of chest, then moves to other side, becoming a W

16 MIDDLETOWN

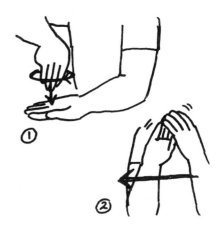

Bent hand circles and touches palm; then B fingertips touch moving to side

‡14 LIMA

L circles

‡19a **TOLEDO**

T taps one side of chest, then taps other side

‡17 **PORTSMOUTH**

P nods

‡19b **TOLEDO**

T traces a 7

‡18a **SPRINGFIELD**

Spell S-P

‡20 **YOUNGSTOWN**

‡18b **SPRINGFIELD**

Spell S-F

Y nods

NOTES

OKLAHOMA

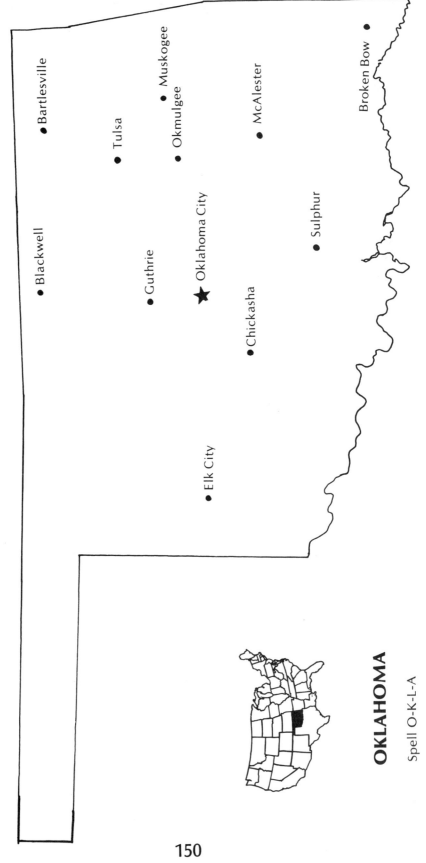

- Bartlesville
- Muskogee
- Tulsa
- Okmulgee
- McAlester
- Broken Bow
- Blackwell
- Guthrie
- Sulphur
- ★ Oklahoma City
- Chickasha
- Elk City

OKLAHOMA

Spell O-K-L-A

1 **BARTLESVILLE**

Spell B-V

4 **CHICKASHA**

2 **BLACKWELL**

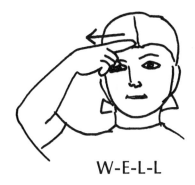

W-E-L-L

G moves from chin to
middle of jaw and back,
opening and closing

Index finger slides
across forehead;
spell W-E-L-L

‡5 **ELK CITY**

Spell E-C

3 **BROKEN BOW**

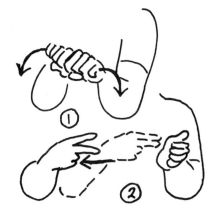

6 **GUTHRIE**

S-hands together
separate arcing down-
ward; H pulls back
from A and opens to V

G traces a 7

7 **McALESTER**

V index slides across
forehead

10 **OKMULGEE**

O touches fingertips,
then heel of palm

‡11 **SULPHUR**

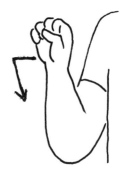

S traces a 7

8 **MUSKOGEE**

M touches fingertips;
then heel of palm

‡12 **TULSA**

T traces a 7

9 **OKLAHOMA CITY** ★

Spell O-C

NOTES

OREGON

OREGON

O circles

Spell O-R-E-G-O-N

Forest Grove
Portland
Beaverton
Oregon City
Salem
Lincoln City
Eugene
North Bend
Medford
Klamath Falls

‡1   **BEAVERTON**

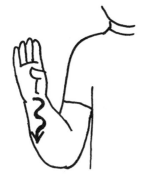

B wiggles down

‡2a   **EUGENE**

E traces a 7

2b   **EUGENE**

E wiggles down

3   **FOREST GROVE**

Spell F-G

4   **KLAMATH FALLS**

Spell K-F

5   **LINCOLN CITY**

C-I-T-Y

L touches temple;
spell C-I-T-Y

6   **MEDFORD**

M wiggles down

7 **NORTH BEND**

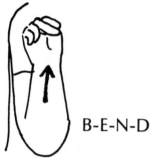

B-E-N-D

Palm-out N moves
up; spell B-E-N-D

‡9 **PORTLAND**

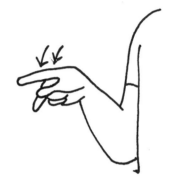

P nods

8 **OREGON CITY**

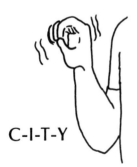

C-I-T-Y

Shake O, spell C-I-T-Y

‡10 **SALEM**

Shake S

NOTES

PENNSYLVANIA

PENNSYLVANIA

Spell P-A

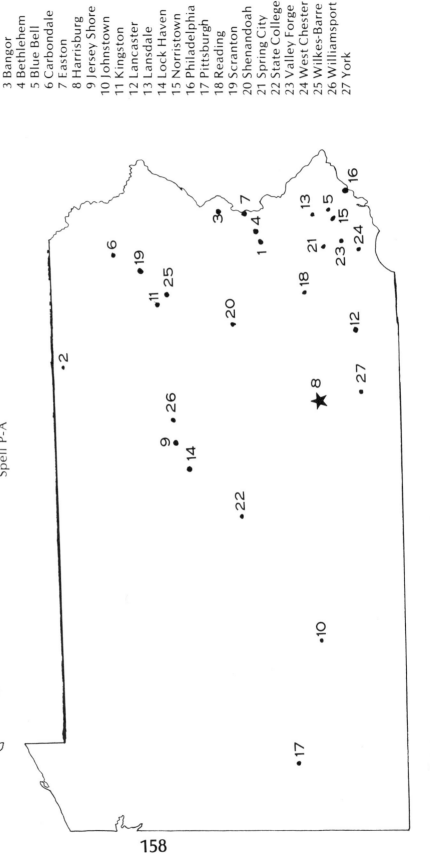

1 Allentown
2 Athens
3 Bangor
4 Bethlehem
5 Blue Bell
6 Carbondale
7 Easton
8 Harrisburg
9 Jersey Shore
10 Johnstown
11 Kingston
12 Lancaster
13 Lansdale
14 Lock Haven
15 Norristown
16 Philadelphia
17 Pittsburgh
18 Reading
19 Scranton
20 Shenandoah
21 Spring City
22 State College
23 Valley Forge
24 West Chester
25 Wilkes-Barre
26 Williamsport
27 York

‡1 ALLENTOWN

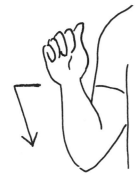

A traces a 7

2 ATHENS

A circles in the
direction of the
thumb

‡3 BANGOR

Shake B

‡4a BETHLEHEM

B circles

‡4b BETHLEHEM

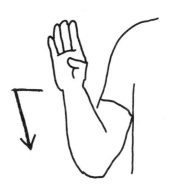

B traces a 7

‡5 BLUE BELL

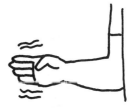

B-E-L-L
Shake B at wrist,
spell **B-E-L-L**

‡6 CARBONDALE

C traces a 7

‡7 EASTON

Shake E

8a HARRISBURG ★

Shake H, fingers
up, palm-in

8b HARRISBURG

H circles, palm-up

†8c HARRISBURG

Nod H, arc to right,
nod again

9 JERSEY SHORE

Spell J-S

10 JOHNSTOWN

Index finger twists
on chin; palm-down X
jerks sharply downward

‡11 KINGSTON

Right K on left shoulder, crosses to right hip

14a LOCK HAVEN

Spell L-H

14b LOCK HAVEN

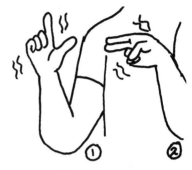

Shake L and H

12 LANCASTER

Shake L

‡15a NORRISTOWN

N circles

‡13 LANSDALE

L circles

‡15b NORRISTOWN

Shake N

‡16   PHILADELPHIA

P traces a 7

‡18b READING

Palm down R nods

‡19   SCRANTON

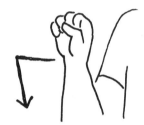

S traces a 7

17   PITTSBURGH

F moves down side of chest, repeat

20   SHENANDOAH

Spell S-H

21   SPRING CITY

‡18a READING

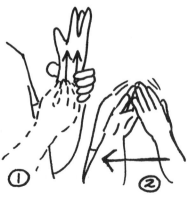

Flat O opens to 5
up through palm-right
C; B taps B moving
sideways

R traces a 7

‡22 STATE COLLEGE

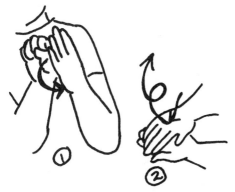

Side of S on finger-tips of left flat palm arcs down to heel; right hand on left, palm to palm; right rises, circling

23 VALLEY FORGE

V-F circles

24 WEST CHESTER

C-H-E-S-T-E-R

W moves to left; spell C-H-E-S-T-E-R

25 WILKES-BARRE

Spell W-B

‡26a WILLIAMSPORT

A-thumb flicks off nose-tip; repeat

26b WILLIAMSPORT

A, palm- left thumb slides down nose several times.

27 YORK

Spell Y-O-R-K downwards

12 Woonsocket

10 Smithfield

5 Lincoln
1 Central Falls
8 Pawtucket

7 North Providence

4 Johnston · 9 Providence · 3 East Providence
2 Cranston

11 Warwick

6 Newport

1 Central Falls
2 Cranston
3 East Providence
4 Johnston
5 Lincoln
6 Newport
7 North Providence
8 Pawtucket
9 Providence
10 Smithfield
11 Warwick
12 Woonsocket

RHODE ISLAND

Spell R-I

RHODE ISLAND

‡1 **CENTRAL FALLS**

Spell C-F

‡2 **CRANSTON**

Shake C

3 **EAST PROVIDENCE**

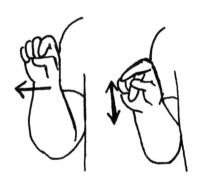

Palm-out E moves
right; P bobs

4 **JOHNSTON**

Spell J-N

‡5 **LINCOLN**

L-thumb taps temple

6 **NEWPORT**

Palm-up right hand
arcs down, brushes across
left palm, and arcs up
slightly; side of 3
on flat palm; both
hands move forward
in slight up-and-down
motion

7   **NORTH PROVIDENCE**

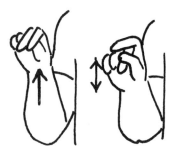

Palm-out N moves
upward; P bobs

10   **SMITHFIELD**

S circles near temple

‡8   **PAWTUCKET**

Index sweeps past
chin

‡11   **WARWICK**

Shake W

‡9   **PROVIDENCE** ★

P bobs

12   **WOONSOCKET**

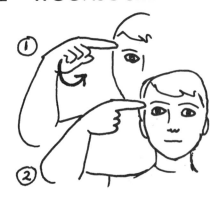

Index twists on temple

NOTES

SOUTH CAROLINA

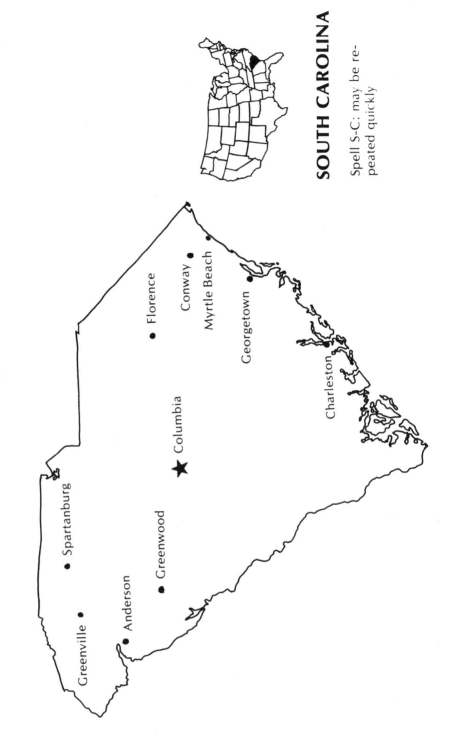

SOUTH CAROLINA

Spell S-C: may be re-
peated quickly

Greenville

Spartanburg

Anderson

Greenwood

Columbia

Florence

Conway

Myrtle Beach

Georgetown

Charleston

‡1 ANDERSON

Shake A

3 COLUMBIA ★

Claw-hand scratches
off left flat O

2a CHARLESTON

C bobs

4 CONWAY

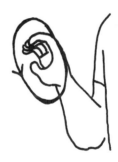

C makes a large
circle

‡2b CHARLESTON

Shake C

‡5 FLORENCE

Shake F

‡6 **GEORGETOWN**

Spell G-T

9 **MYRTLE BEACH**

Spell M-B

‡7 **GREENVILLE**

G circles

‡10a **SPARTANBURG**

S circles **slightly**

‡8 **GREENWOOD**

Shake G

‡10b **SPARTANBURG**

Shake S

170

NOTES

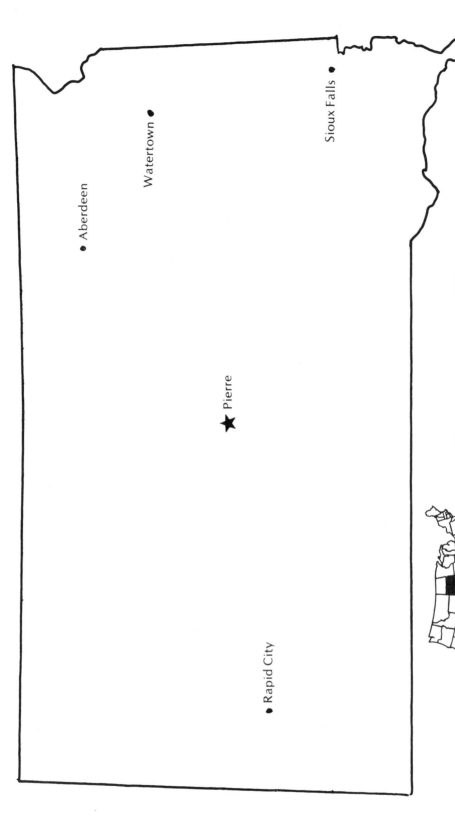

SOUTH DAKOTA

Aberdeen •

Watertown •

Sioux Falls •

Pierre ★

Rawpid City •

SOUTH DAKOTA

Spell S-D

‡1 ABERDEEN

A taps temple

‡4 SIOUX FALLS ★

Spell S-F

5 WATERTOWN

Index finger of palm-left W taps chin; finger-tips touch at left; separate, touch at right

‡2 PIERRE

P circles and touches temple

3 RAPID CITY

Spell R-C

TENNESSEE

TENNESSEE

Spell T-F-N-N

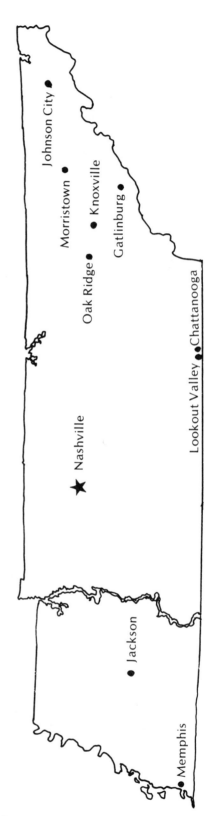

- Johnson City
- Morristown
- Knoxville
- Oak Ridge
- Gatlinburg
- Lookout Valley
- Chattanooga
- ★ Nashville
- Jackson
- Memphis

1a CHATTANOOGA

Spell C-H-A-T-T

1b CHATTANOOGA

C brushes off palm

2 GATLINBURG

G arcs down on to back of hand; B arcs down on to back of palm

‡3 JACKSON

J brushes off top of S

‡4 JOHNSON CITY

Spell J-C

‡5 KNOXVILLE

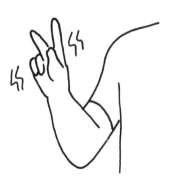

Shake K

6   LOOKOUT VALLEY

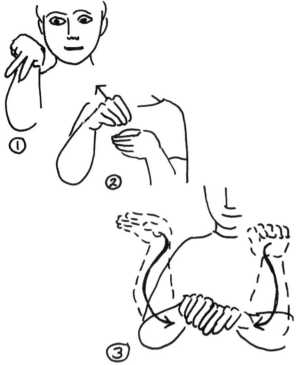

V hands, tips out,
move from side of eye;
bent hand moves up
out of palm-right C;
open hands arc down
to touch

7   MEMPHIS

M brushes off heel
of palm

‡8   MORRISTOWN

Shake M

9   NASHVILLE ★

N circles at temple
and touches temple

‡10   OAK RIDGE

Spell O-R

176

NOTES

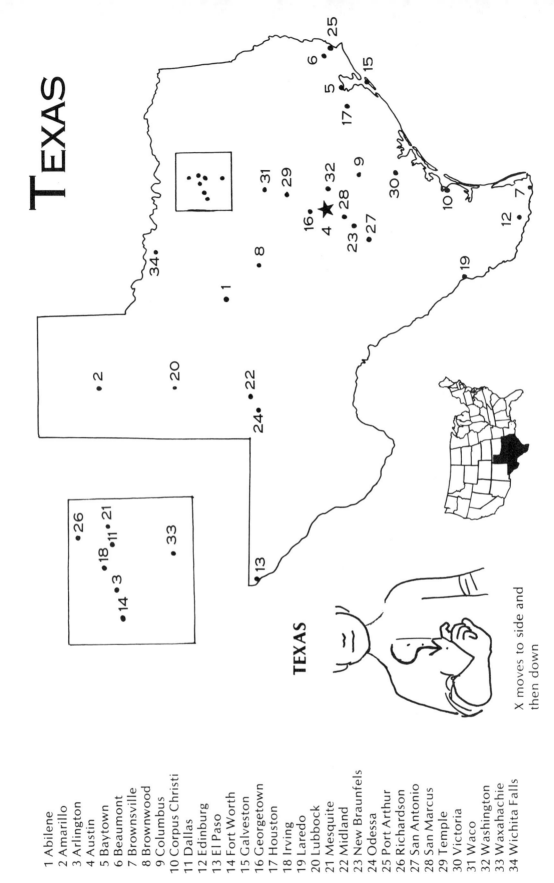

Texas

TEXAS

X moves to side and then down

1 Abilene
2 Amarillo
3 Arlington
4 Austin
5 Baytown
6 Beaumont
7 Brownsville
8 Brownwood
9 Columbus
10 Corpus Christi
11 Dallas
12 Edinburg
13 El Paso
14 Fort Worth
15 Galveston
16 Georgetown
17 Houston
18 Irving
19 Laredo
20 Lubbock
21 Mesquite
22 Midland
23 New Braunfels
24 Odessa
25 Port Arthur
26 Richardson
27 San Antonio
28 San Marcus
29 Temple
30 Victoria
31 Waco
32 Washington
33 Waxahachie
34 Wichita Falls

‡1 ABILENE

A taps forehead

3 ARLINGTON

A taps center of palm

2a AMARILLO

A touches palm and
weaves **away from hand**

‡4a AUSTIN ★

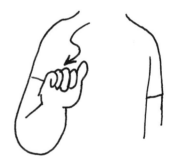

A **traces** an S

2b AMARILLO

A thumb taps palm-
right B

‡4b AUSTIN

A bobs

179

‡4c AUSTIN

A traces a 7

‡7 BROWNSVILLE

B taps center of palm

5 BAYTOWN

B circles in front
of nose

8 BROWNWOOD

Slide B down face; saw
on palm-down hand

6 BEAUMONT

B fingertips tap cheek

9 COLUMBUS

C circles forward
from shoulder

‡10 CORPUS CHRISTI

Nod C, arc to right,
nod again

11 DALLAS

D taps temple

12 EDINBURG

E taps center of palm

13a EL PASO

E passes L

13b EL PASO

L passes O

14 FORT WORTH

F and W tap center
of palm

181

15 GALVESTON

Thumb of G taps
corner of mouth

‡16 GEORGETOWN

Spell G-T

17 HOUSTON

H-index taps corner
of mouth

‡18 IRVING

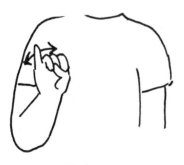

Shake I

19 LAREDO

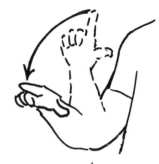

L arcs down
from shoulder

20 LUBBOCK

L taps temple

‡21 MESQUITE

M taps temple

22 MIDLAND

M circles and touches
back of flat palm-
down hand

‡23 NEW BRAUNFELS

Spell N-B

24 ODESSA

O taps back of
S-hand

‡25 PORT ARTHUR

Spell P-A

26 RICHARDSON

R taps temple

27 SAN ANTONIO

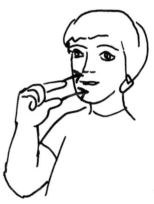

G-fingertips tap
corner of mouth

28 SAN MARCOS

Spell S-M

‡29 TEMPLE

Heel of T touches
back of S-hand

30 VICTORIA

V-index taps heel
of flat hand

31 WACO

W-index taps
heel of flat hand

‡32 WASHINGTON

W circles forward
from shoulder

33 WAXAHACHIE

W-index taps temple
twice

34 WICHITA FALLS

W and F tap center
of flat hand

NOTES

Uᴛᴀʜ

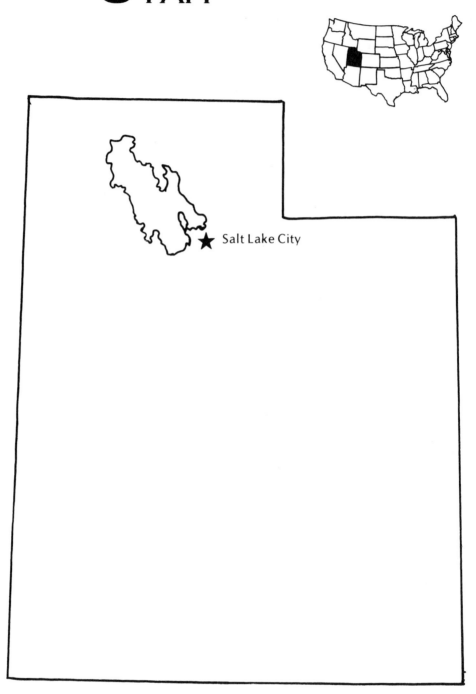

★ Salt Lake City

UTAH

U circles forward

UTAH

Spell U-T-A-H

SALT LAKE CITY

Spell S-L-C

Essex Junction

Burlington

★ Montpelier

● Chelsea

White River Junction ●

● Rutland

Vermont

Springfield ●

Manchester ●

Bellow Falls ●

Wilmington ●

Bennington ●

● Brattleboro

● Whitingham

VERMONT

Spell V-T

Vermont

1 BELLOWS FALLS

Spell B-F

2 BENNINGTON

Spell B-E-N-N

‡3 BRATTLEBORO

Nod B, arc to right,
nod again

‡4 BURLINGTON

B traces a 7

‡5 CHELSEA

Shake C

6 ESSEX JUNCTION

S-hands crossed
at wrists, shake

‡7 MANCHESTER

Shake M

‡8 MONTPELIER ★

Index finger circles
and touches temple

189

‡9 RUTLAND

Shake R

‡10 SPRINGFIELD

Shake S

11 WHITE RIVER JUNCTION

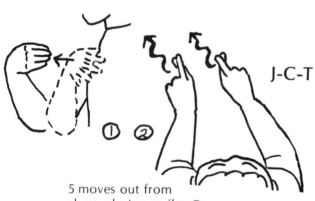

J-C-T

5 moves out from chest, closing to flat-O; parallel R's ripple out from body; spell J-C-T

12 WHITINGHAM

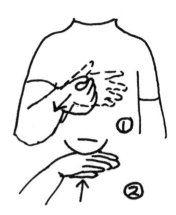

5 moves out from chest, closing to flat-O; palm-down B moves from chest up to chin

‡13 WILMINGTON

W traces a 7

190

NOTES

Virginia

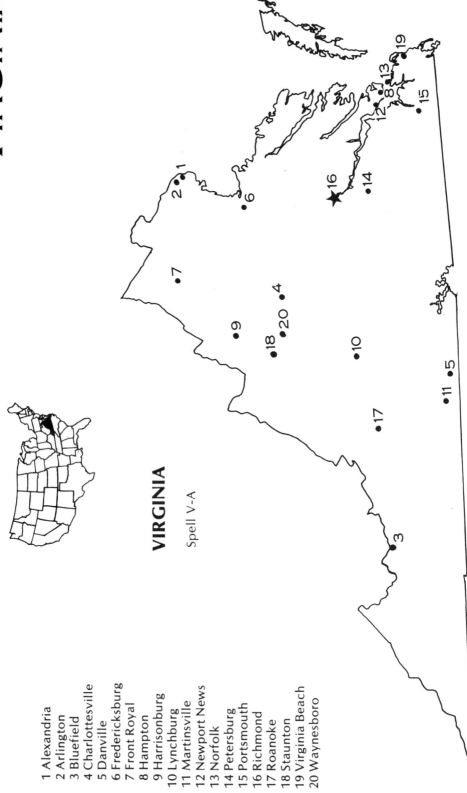

VIRGINIA

Spell V-A

1 Alexandria
2 Arlington
3 Bluefield
4 Charlottesville
5 Danville
6 Fredericksburg
7 Front Royal
8 Hampton
9 Harrisonburg
10 Lynchburg
11 Martinsville
12 Newport News
13 Norfolk
14 Petersburg
15 Portsmouth
16 Richmond
17 Roanoke
18 Staunton
19 Virginia Beach
20 Waynesboro

‡1 ALEXANDRIA

Spell A-L-E-X

2 ARLINGTON

Spell A-R-L

5 DANVILLE

3 BLUEFIELD

F-I-E-L-D

Palm-left B shakes
from wrist; spell **F-I-E-L-D**

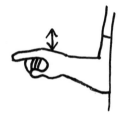

D, palm-down, bobs

4 CHARLOTTESVILLE

C-thumb taps shoulder

6a FREDERICKSBURG

F, palm-up, moves
out and back slightly

‡6b FREDERICKSBURG

Shake F

7 FRONT ROYAL

Spell F-R

8 HAMPTON

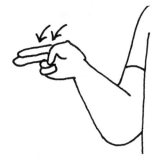

H nods, palm left

9 HARRISONBURG

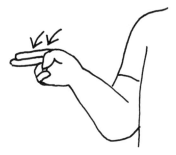

H nods, palm left

10 LYNCHBURG

L, palm left, shakes
at temple

I1 MARTINSVILLE

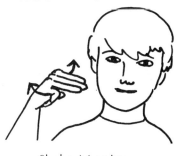

Shake M at jaw,
palm left

12 NEWPORT NEWS

Spell N-N, moving
to the right

‡13a NORFOLK

Shake N

‡13b NORFOLK

Shake N at jaw,
palm left

‡13c NORFOLK

Shake N at temple

14 PETERSBURG

Shake P

15 PORTSMOUTH

P shakes at jaw,
fingertips pointing
at jaw

16a RICHMOND ★

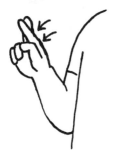

R nods

‡16b RICHMOND

Shake R

‡16c RICHMOND

R traces a 7

‡17 ROANOKE

R points down
and circles

‡18 STAUNTON

S traces a 7

‡19 VIRGINIA BEACH

Spell V-B

20 WAYNESBORO

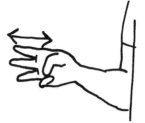

W, fingertips out,
palm left, moves forward
and back several
times

NOTES

Spokane •

• Walla Walla

• Ellensburg

• Yakima

• White Salmon

Bellingham

• Mount Vernon

Everett
Seattle
• Bellevue
Tacoma
Puyallup

• Centralia
• Chehalis

Vancouver

Olympia

Long Beach

Port Angeles

WASHINGTON

W, from shoulder, circles forward

WASHINGTON STATE

198

‡1 BELLEVUE

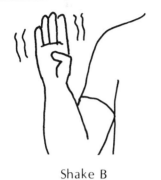

Shake B

‡2 BELLINGHAM

Shake B

3a CENTRALIA

Palm-down extended-A
hand rotates above left
palm and touches
center of palm

‡3b CENTRALIA

Shake C

‡4 CHEHALIS

Spell C-S

‡5a ELLENSBURG

Shake E

‡5b ELLENSBURG

Spell E-L

199

‡6 **EVERETT**

Shake E

‡9 **OLYMPIA** ★

Shake O

‡10 **PORT ANGELES**

Spell P-A

‡7 **LONG BEACH**

Spell L-B

11 **PUYALLUP**

Spell P-Y-L

8a **MOUNT VERNON**

Spell M-V

‡12 **SEATTLE**

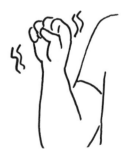

Shake S

8b **MOUNT VERNON**

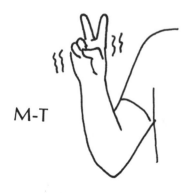

M-T

Spell M-T; shake V

200

‡13 **SPOKANE**

Spell S-P

‡14 TACOMA

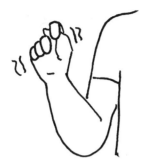

Shake T

17 WHITE SALMON

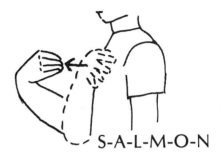

S-A-L-M-O-N

5 on chest moves out-
ward, closing to a flat-O;
spell S-A-L-M-O-N

‡15 VANCOUVER

Shake V

‡18a YAKIMA

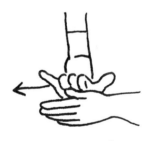

Palm-down Y slides
off left palm

16 WALLA WALLA

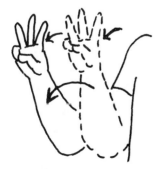

W nods, arc to right,
nod again

18b YAKIMA

Shake Y

WASHINGTON, D. C.
(DISTRICT OF COLUMBIA)

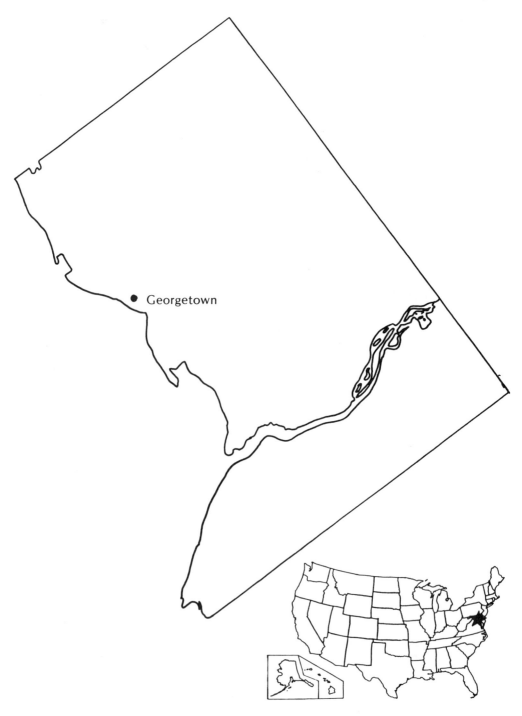

● Georgetown

GEORGETOWN

Spell G-T

WASHINGTON, D.C.

D-C

Palm-in W from shoulder
circles forward and right;
spell D-C

WEST VIRGINIA

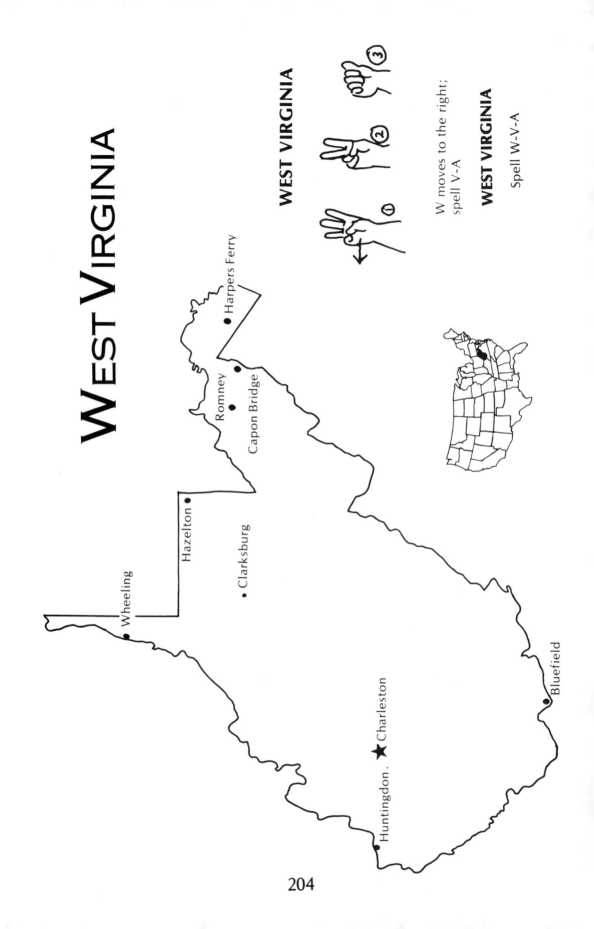

Wheeling •

Hazelton •

• Clarksburg

Romney •

Capon Bridge •

• Harpers Ferry

Huntingdon •

★ Charleston

• Bluefield

WEST VIRGINIA

① ② ③

W moves to the right;
spell V-A

WEST VIRGINIA

Spell W-V-A

2 CAPON BRIDGE

‡1a BLUEFIELD

B traces a 7

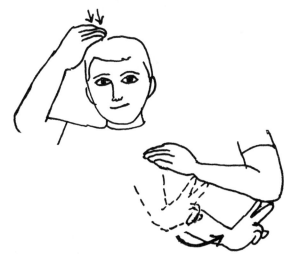

Tap top of head
with open-hand finger-
tips; fingertips of V
touch left palm, arc
to touch arm near
elbow

1b BLUEFIELD

B swings to side
several times, moving
down

‡3a CHARLESTON ★

Shake C at ear
level, palm left

205

3b CHARLESTON

C brushes down side
of cheek several
times

5 HARPERS FERRY

Spell H-F

4a CLARKSBURG

C wiggles down
from ear

6 HAZELTON

H circles, palm up,
near face

4b CLARKSBURG

C index & thumb
tap palm-right B

‡7a HUNTINGTON

Nod H, arc to right,
nod again

7b HUNTINGTON

H, palm in, bobs

9a WHEELING

W wiggles down
from ear

7c HUNTINGTON

H wiggles down
from ear

9b WHEELING

W circles in a
large circle

‡8 ROMNEY

R taps back of
S-hand

Wisconsin

WISCONSIN

Spell W-I-S-C

1 Appleton
2 Burlington
3 Delavan
4 Eau Claire
5 Elkhorn
6 Fond du Lac
7 Green Bay
8 Institute
9 Kenosha
10 La Crosse
11 Lake Geneva
12 Madison
13 Menomonee Falls
14 Milwaukee
15 Oak Creek
16 Oshkosh
17 Racine
18 Sheboygan
19 Sun Prairie
20 Wausau

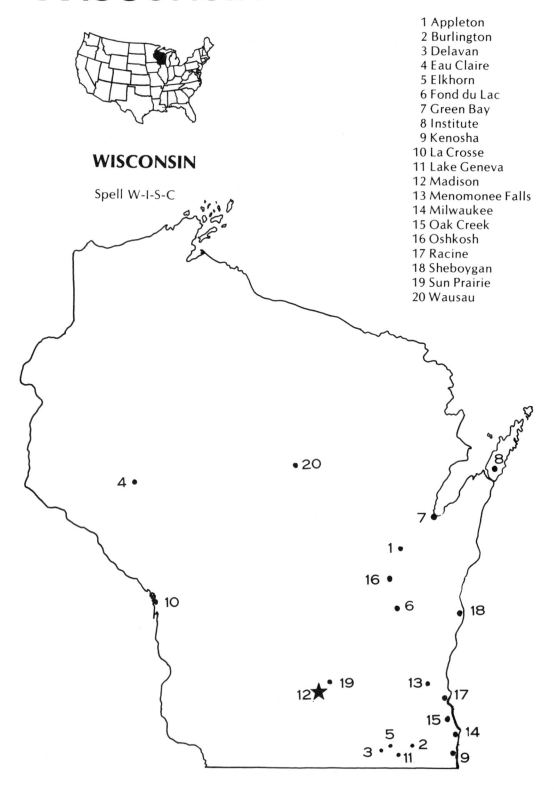

‡1 APPLETON

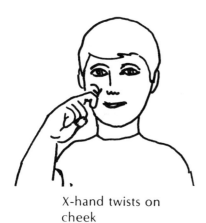

X-hand twists on cheek

‡2 BURLINGTON

B traces a 7

‡3 DELAVAN

Shake D

‡4 EAU CLAIRE

Spell E-C

5 ELKHORN

Thumb of 5-hand touches side of head twice

6 FOND DU LAC

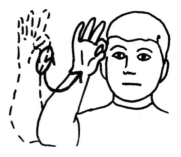

F circles at temple and touches temple

†7 GREEN BAY

Spell G-B

‡8 **INSTITUTE**

Side of right I
taps on index-side
of left I

‡12 **MADISON** ★

M circles at temple
and touches temple

‡13 **MENOMONEE FALLS**

Tap nose with index
slightly

9 **KENOSHA**

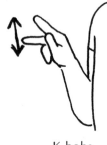

K bobs

10 **LA CROSSE**

Spell L-A-X

14 **MILWAUKEE**

Index slides across
chin several times

‡11 **LAKE GENEVA**

Spell L-G

‡15 OAK CREEK

Spell O-C

‡18a SHEBOYGAN

V fingers close and open while moving up arm

‡16 OSHKOSH

Shake O

18b SHEBOYGAN

S moves up arm

‡19 SUN PRAIRIE

Spell S-P

‡17 RACINE

R bobs

‡20 WAUSAU

W bobs

WYOMING

Map showing cities in Wyoming:
- Evanston
- Thermopolis
- Riverton
- Lander
- Buffalo
- Gillette
- Casper
- Wheatland
- Laramie
- ★ Cheyenne

WYOMING

W hands, palm-out, arc down to sides, changing to Y-hands

212

Wyoming

‡1 BUFFALO

Y palm-in touches
mid-forehead

2 CASPER

Elbow of right C
on left hand, arm nods
back and forth

3 CHEYENNE ★

C-thumb slides over
head, front to back

4 EVANSTON

E, palm left, circles
forward on side of
head

‡5 GILLETTE

Draw thumb of Y
along cheek twice

6 LANDER

Palm-out L on
knuckles of palm-down
left A

213

7 LARAMIE

Palm-out L weaves down

9 THERMOPOLIS

Palm-in T at mouth;
twist downward and to
side

8 RIVERTON

Palm-down R wiggles
down.

10 WHEATLAND

W-index on each side
of chin; then palm-up
O sideways closing to A

NOTES

CANADA

(CANADIAN SIGNS)

CANADA

A-hand grabs side of
chest

CANADA

A-hand, palm in, moves
up and down chest
several times

PROVINCE

P makes a cross on heart

CANADA

C-hand makes large arc
to side

ALBERTA

ALBERTA

Spell A-L-T-A

ALBERTA

‡ A shakes

ALBERTA

A, palm-down, brushes off back of palm-down S several times

ALBERTA

Front side of A touches chin and rocks

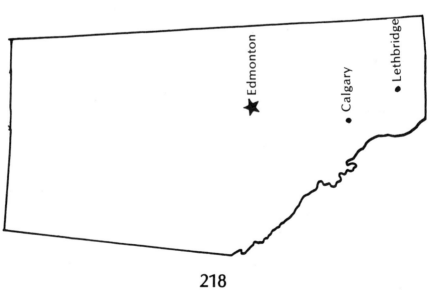

★ Edmonton

• Calgary

• Lethbridge

2b   **EDMONTON**

E, palm in, touches
nose

‡1a   **CALGARY**

C shakes

‡2c   **EDMONTON**

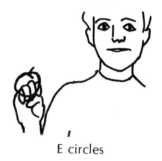

E circles

‡1b   **CALGARY**

L hands point at
angles upward and
rotate alternately up
and down at wrists

3   **LETHBRIDGE**

L-E-T-H

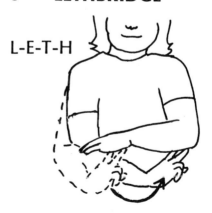

Spell L-E-T-H, then V
hand arcs under fore-
arm of palm-down
hand, making contact
at the wrist, then elbow

2a   **EDMONTON** ★

Spell E-D

British Columbia

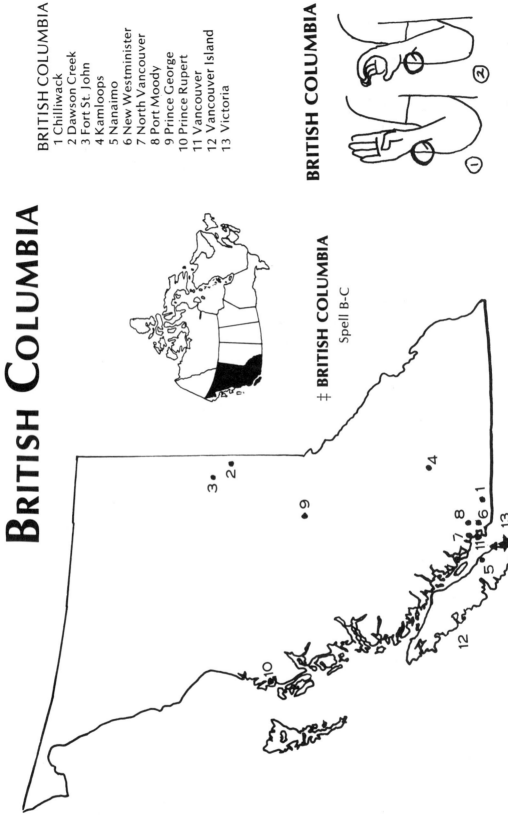

BRITISH COLUMBIA

1 Chilliwack
2 Dawson Creek
3 Fort St. John
4 Kamloops
5 Nanaimo
6 New Westminister
7 North Vancouver
8 Port Moody
9 Prince George
10 Prince Rupert
11 Vancouver
12 Vancouver Island
13 Victoria

BRITISH COLUMBIA

B circles, C circles

‡ **BRITISH COLUMBIA**
Spell B-C

‡ 1 **CHILLIWACK**

C shakes

2 **DAWSON CREEK**

Spell D-C

3 **FORT ST. JOHN**

Spell F-T-S-J

4 **KAMLOOPS**

Bent V taps straight
at mouth

5 **NANAIMO**

N taps thumb side of
palm-right S

6 **NEW WESTMINSTER**

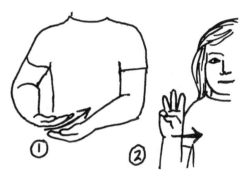

Flat hand, palm up,
sweeps through other
flat hand, palm up,
then W moves to left

7 **NORTH VANCOUVER**

N moves upward, then
V shakes

‡8   **PORT   MOODY**

Spell P-M

‡11a **VANCOUVER**

Shake V

9   **PRINCE GEORGE**

Spell P-G on chest

11b **VANCOUVER**

Shake V in wide arc

11c **VANCOUVER**

Spell V-A-N

10   **PRINCE RUPERT**

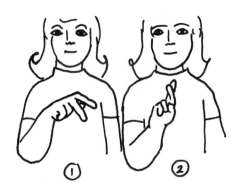

Spell P-R on chest

12   **VANCOUVER ISLAND**

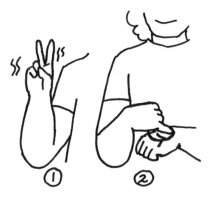

Shake V, then little-
finger-side of I circles
on back of S

13a **VICTORIA** ★

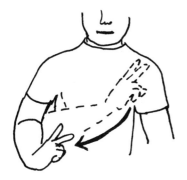

V touches shoulder,
then arcs to waist on
opposite side

13c **VICTORIA**

V traces a 7

13b **VICTORIA**

V shakes very slightly

MANITOBA

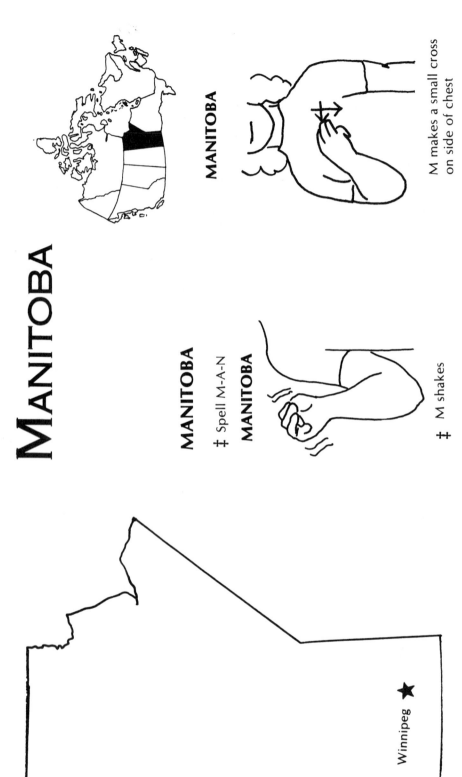

MANITOBA

‡ Spell M-A-N

MANITOBA

‡ M shakes

MANITOBA

M makes a small cross on side of chest

Winnipeg ★

‡1a **WINNIPEG** ★

W, palm in, circles
vertically

1c **WINNIPEG**

W hands, crossed,
bend at wrist

1b **WINNIPEG**

W, palm up - shakes

Fredericton

Saint John

‡ **NEW BRUNSWICK**

Spell N-B

‡ **FREDERICTON**

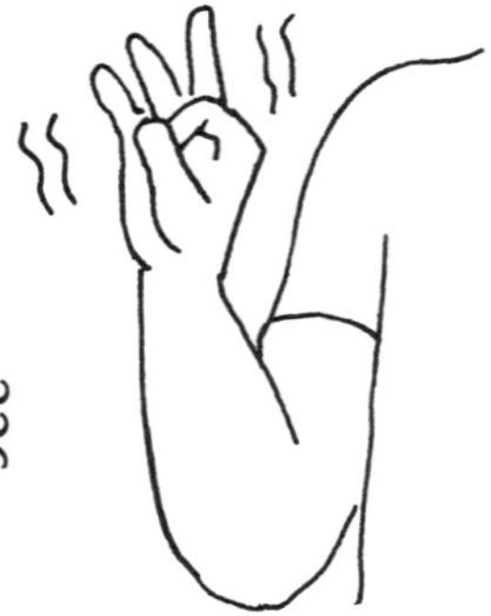

F shakes

‡ **ST. JOHN**

Spell S-T-J

ST. JOHN

S at shoulder arcs to become J on back of wrist

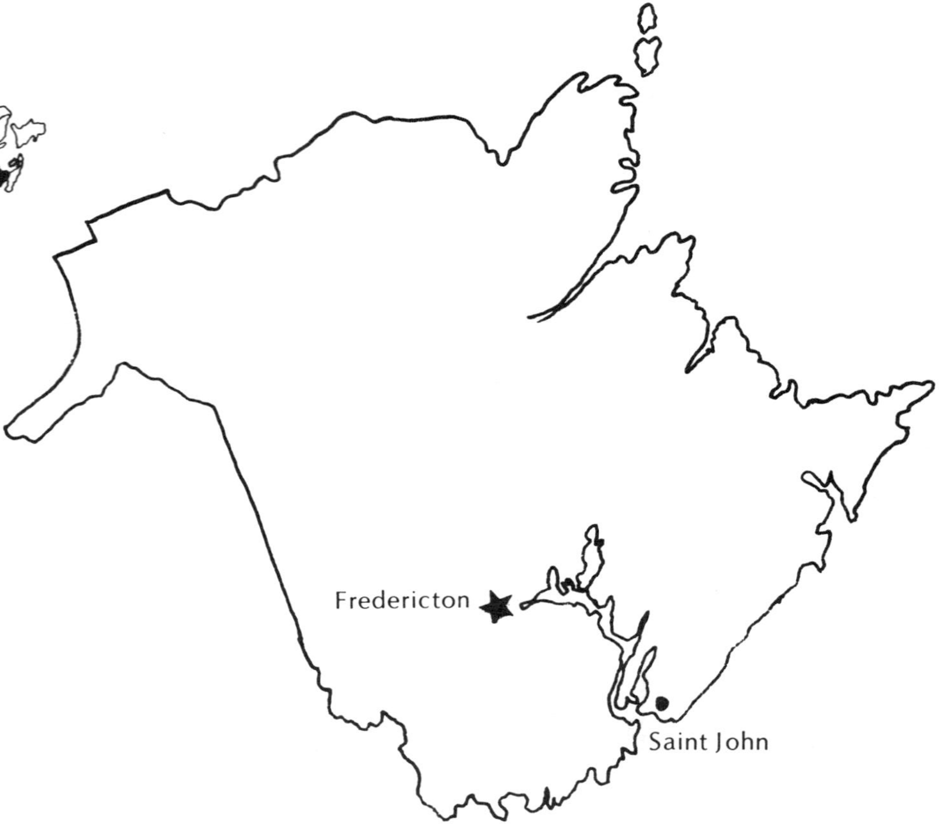

NEW BRUNSWICK

NEWFOUNDLAND

Spell N-F-L-D

NEWFOUNDLAND

Open B hands at waist,
bend several times

‡ ST. JOHNS

Spell S-T-J

St. John's

NEWFOUNDLAND

NORTHWEST TERRITORIES

NORTHWEST TERRITORIES

Spell N-W-T

‡YELLOW KNIFE

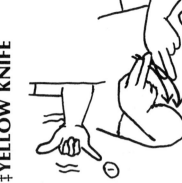

Y rotates at wrist, H flicks off H several times

★ Yellowknife

NOTES

NOVA SCOTIA

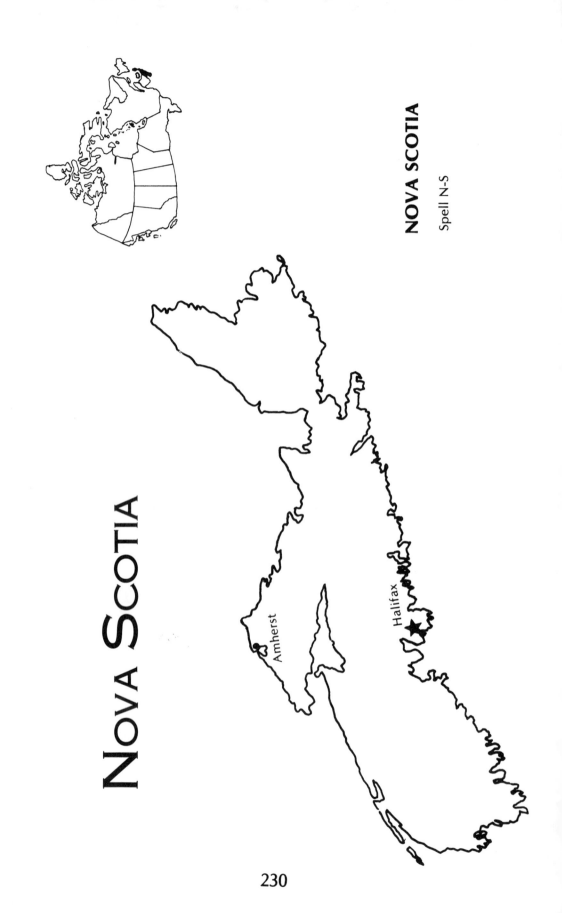

Amherst

Halifax

NOVA SCOTIA

Spell N-S

1   **AMHERST**

Flat hand, palm in,
moves in front of
mouth several times

2b   **HALIFAX**

Closed C slides to side
off chin and closes,
repeat

2a   **HALIFAX** ★

H sweeps to side off
chin several times

2c   **HALIFAX**

Claw hand scratches
down chin, repeat

ONTARIO
1 Belleville
2 Hamilton
3 Kitchener
4 London
5 North Bay
6 Ottawa
7 Sudbury
8 Thunder Bay
9 Toronto
10 Windsor

ONTARIO

ONTARIO

‡   O shakes

ONTARIO

O, palm in, circles vertically

ONTARIO

‡   O, palm out, circles vertically

ONTARIO

O, palm in, circles horizontally

1   BELLVILLE

B on fingers of left flat hand
traces a 7

4   LONDON

L touches chin, then
moves to touch center
of chest

2   HAMILTON

G hand at eye level,
palm out, moves to
side and closes

3   KITCHENER

K touches chin then
moves to touch side of
chest

‡ 5a NORTH BAY

Spell N-B

5b NORTH BAY

B-A-Y

N moves upward, spell B-A-Y

5c NORTH BAY

N moves upward, spell B

6a OTTAWA

O, palm out, circles horizontally

‡ 6b OTTAWA

O traces a 7

‡ 6c OTTAWA

O nods, arcs to side and nods again

7a SUDBURY

S, palm in, circles vertically

7b SUDBURY

S, palm to side, circles vertically at side of head

8a THUNDER BAY

Spell T-B

8b THUNDER BAY

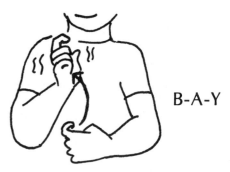

B-A-Y

X hands, one above the other, top X moves upward shaking, spell B-A-Y

‡9 TORONTO ★

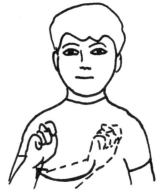

T taps one side of chest, arcs to tap other side; may be done with bent flat hand

10 WINDSOR

Palm-out W bobs and arcs to side slightly

NOTES

PRINCE EDWARD
ISLAND

**PRINCE EDWARD
ISLAND**

Spell P-E-I

NOTES

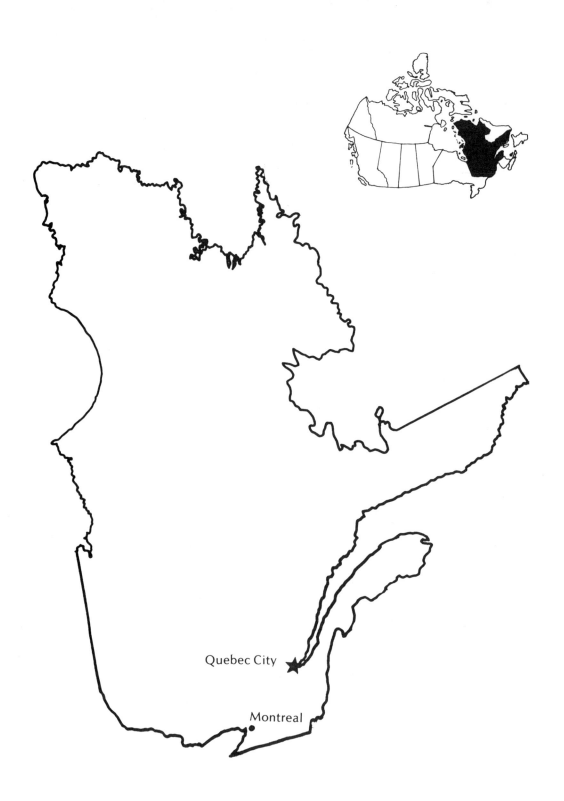

Quebec City ★

Montreal •

QUEBEC

QUEBEC

Q circles horizontally

QUEBEC

Q shakes

QUEBEC CITY

Q circles horizontally,
flat hands tap at fingers

‡ MONTREAL

M circles to touch
palm-up flat hand

MONTREAL

M touches side of head
and moves to touch
palm

SASKATCHEWAN

SASKATCHEWAN

Spell S-A-S-K

SASKATCHEWAN

Spell S-K on side of head

‡ PRINCE ALBERT

Spell P-A

‡ REGINA

R traces a 7

REGINA

R touches side of thumb-up S, then moves to side and down

Regina

Prince Albert ★

Yukon Territory

WHITE HORSE

5 pulls out to flat-O from chest, H with thumb spread touches side of head, and index and middle finger bend

YUKON

Spell Y-U-K-O-N

★ Whitehorse

MEXICO
(MEXICAN SIGNS)

Tijuana

Ciudad Juarez

Chihuahua

Ciudad Obregon

Piedras Negras

Durango

Ciudad Victoria

Monterrey

San Luis Potosi

Guadalajara

Leon

Queretaro

Mexico City

Toluca

Puebla

Veracruz

Oaxaca

Acapulco

MEXICO

MEXICO

Index of V touches
center of head, moves
out and slightly down
with a flick of the wrist

MEXICO

(American Sign)

Index on shoulder drops
to palm-up X

MEXICO

(American Sign)

M fingertips trace mustache

MEXICO

(American Sign)

M fingertips brush lower cheek
several times

1 ACAPULCO

A at ear-level moves out and back while twisting slightly

2 CHIHUAHUA

E at mouth-level turns and becomes H, fingers up, touching mouth

3 CIUDAD JUAREZ

A-hand with thumb extended circles to touch palm-up flat hand, then A slides across lips

4 CIUDAD OBREGON

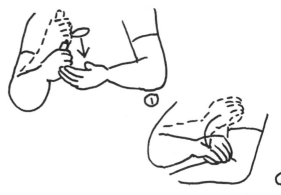

A-hand with thumb extended circles to touch palm-up flat hand, then O arcs from shoulder to elbow

5 CIUDAD VICTORIA

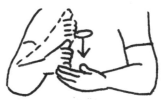

V-I-C-T-O-R-I-A

A-hand with thumb extended circles to touch palm-up flat hand, then spell V-I-C-T-O-R-I-A

6 DURANGO

D, fingertips towards ear, rotates at wrist

7 GUADALAJARA

G, at ear level, moves
out and back while
twisting slightly

8 LEON

Claw hand moves down
side of face

9 MEXICO CITY ★

Index of V touches
center of head, moves
out and slightly down
with a flick of the
wrist

10 MONTERREY

M, in center of fore-
head, fingers pointing
out, fingers move up
and down

11 OAXACA

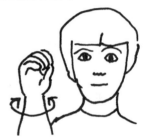

O, fingertips toward
ear, rotates at wrist

12 PIEDRAS NEGRAS

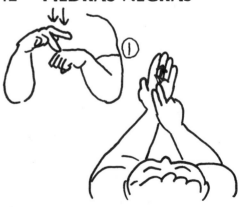

P taps back of A, then
N rubs forward on
palm-up flat hand

13 PUEBLA

P, fingertips toward ear, rotates at wrist

16 TIJUANA

T and I on same hand, twist downward at wrists

14 QUERETERO

Bent L with index and thumb pointing to ear, rotates at wrist

17 TOLUCA

Right F on left shoulder, then heart

15 SAN LUIS POTOSI

P circles and touches side of head

18 VERACRUZ

V, fingertips toward ear, rotates at wrist

APPENDIX A

LINGUISTIC NOTES

Sample

Forty-one informants in 31 states responded to a paper and pencil survey which requested descriptions for signs that name cities in their state, and 310 informants were interviewed.

Methodology

An initial corpus of data was collected in personal interviews and by means of a paper and pencil survey sent to individuals associated with the state residential school or the state association of the deaf. After this corpus was collected, the *direct questioning* method (Wolfram and Fasold, 1974) was used to confirm the data. Deaf informants were presented a written description of signs collected for their "home" state. They then signed them according to the written description. If the sign produced by the informant was not the one intended by the written description, the sign was shown to the informant by the interviewer. The informant then stated whether he uses or sees other deaf people use that sign. If the informant did not use that particular sign, the interviewer asked for the sign used by the informant and recorded it. In order to obtain further data, *structural elicitation* (Wolfram and Fasold, 1974), using a map of the informant's "home" state or country was employed. The informant was then asked if he knew signs for any of the other cities on the stimulus map. A paper and pencil transcription was used to record the data. All data used in this text were collected by the authors. Data for Canadian and Mexican cities were collected and confirmed in personal interviews using the techniques of structural elicitation and direct questioning as described above.

Some Abbreviation Rules Based on American Data

Some of the data in this text consist of fingerspelled components which appear to be English abbreviations. LOS ANGELES (L-A), appears to be derived from the common speech abbreviation *l-a* (see note 1). CONNECTICUT (C-O-N-N) and FLORIDA (F-L-A) may have originated from the printed abbreviations "Conn." and "Fla." However, other data suggest that different types of abbreviation rules may also be present. That is, signers form abbreviations as if they were following these rules.

1. Names which are composed of separate words are signed using the handshapes for the initial letters of each word.
   a. Abbreviations to two handshapes
      i. Two words in print

FORT SMITH, Ark.	F-S	COLORADO SPRINGS, Co.	C-S
LITTLE ROCK, Ark.	L-R	FORT COLLINS, Co.	F-C
PINE BLUFF, Ark.	P-B	GLENWOOD SPRINGS, Co.	G-S
EL DORADO, Ark.	E-D	GRAND JUNCTION, Co.	G-J
LAKE TAHOE, Ca.	L-T	WOODLAND PARK, Co.	W-P
LONG BEACH, Ca.	L-B	WEST HARTFORD, Conn.	W-H
LOS ANGELES, Ca.	L-A	CAMDEN-WYOMING, Del.	C-W
SAN DIEGO, Ca.	S-D	DEWEY BEACH, Del.	D-B
SAN JOSE, Ca.	S-J	NEW CASTLE, Del.	N-C
VAN NUYS, Ca.	V-N	DAYTONA BEACH, Fla.	D-B
WOODLAND HILLS, Ca.	W-H	PANAMA CITY, Fla.	P-C

CAVE SPRING, Ga.	C-S		LAS CRUCES, N.M.	L-C
COLLEGE PARK, Ga.	C-P		LAS VEGAS, N.M.	L-V
FOREST PARK, Ga.	F-P		LOS ALAMOS, N.M.	L-A
PEARL CITY, Hi.	P-C		SANTA FE, N.M.	S-F
PEARL HARBOR,Hi.	P-H		GLEN FALLS, N.Y.	G-F
GLENNS FERRY, Id.	G-F		LAKE GEORGE, N.Y.	L-G
GRAND VIEW, Id.	G-V		LAKE PLACID, N.Y.	L-P
IDAHO FALLS, Id.	I-F		LONG ISLAND, N.Y.	L-I
NEW PLYMOUTH, Id.	N-P		NIAGARA FALLS, N.Y.	N-F
POST FALLS, Id.	P-F		STATEN ISLAND, N.Y.	S-I
ARLINGTON HEIGHTS, Ill	A-H		CHAPEL HILL, N.C.	C-H
FORT WAYNE, Ind.	F-W		ROCKY MOUNT, N.C.	R-M
SOUTH BEND, Ind.	S-B		WAKE FOREST, N.C.	W-F
TERRE HAUTE, Ind.	T-H		WINSTON-SALEM, N.C.	W-S
CEDAR FALLS, Io.	C-F		DEVIL'S LAKE, N.D.	D-L
CEDAR RAPIDS, Io.	C-R		GRAND FORKS, N.D.	G-F
COUNCIL BLUFF, Io.	C-B		ELK CITY, Okla.	E-C
DES MOINES, Io	D-M		OKLAHOMA CITY, Okla.	O-C
FORT DODGE, Io.	F-D		FOREST GROVE, Ore.	F-G
GRAND MOUND, Io.	G-M		KLAMATH FALLS, Ore.	K-F
SIOUX CITY, Io.	S-C		JERSEY SHORE, Ore.	J-S
JUNCTION CITY, Kan.	J-C		LOCK HAVEN, Ore.	L-H
KANSAS CITY, Kan.	K-C		WILKES-BARRE, Pa.	W-B
OVERLAND PARK, Kan.	O-P		CENTRAL FALLS, R.I.	C-F
BOWLING GREEN, Ky.	B-G		MYRTLE BEACH, S.C.	M-B
BATON ROUGE, La.	B-R		RAPID CITY, S.D.	R-C
DENHAM SPRINGS, La.	D-S		SIOUX FALLS, S.D.	S-F
LAKE CHARLES, La.	L-C		JOHNSON CITY, Tenn.	J-C
VILLE PLATTE, La.	V-P		OAKRIDGE, Tenn.	O-R
LEWISTON-AUBURN, Me.	L-A		NEW BRAUNFELS, Tex.	N-B
PRESQUE ISLE, Me.	P-I		PORT ARTHUR, Tex.	P-A
OCEAN CITY, Md.	O-C		SAN MARCOS, Tex.	S-M
POCOMOKE CITY, Md.	P-C		BELLOW FALLS, Vt.	B-F
BATTLE CREEK, Mich.	B-C		FRONT ROYAL, Va.	F-R
GARDEN CITY, Mich.	G-C		VIRGINIA BEACH, Va.	V-B
GRAND BLANC, Mich.	G-B		LONG BEACH, Wash.	L-B
GRAND RAPIDS, Mich.	G-R		MOUNT VERNON, Wash.	M-V
HOUGHTON LAKE, Mich.	H-L		PORT ANGELES, Wash.	P-A
PORT HURON, Mich.	P-H		HARPER'S FERRY, W.Va.	H-F
SWARTZ CREEK, Mich.	S-C		EAU CLAIRE, Wis.	E-C
TRAVERSE CITY, Mich.	T-C		GREEN BAY, Wis.	G-B
WOODLAND PARK, Mich.	W-P		LAKE GENEVA, Wis.	L-G
ALBERT LEA, Minn.	A-L		OAK CREEK, Wis.	O-C
LITTLE FALLS, Minn.	L-F		SUN PRAIRIE, Wis.	S-P
SAUK CENTRE, Minn.	S-C			
JEFFERSON CITY, Mo.	J-C			
KANSAS CITY, Mo.	K-C		ii. Compound Words	
UNIVERSITY CITY, Mo.	U-C		BAKERSFIELD, Ca.	B-F
GREAT FALLS, Mont.	G-F		GEORGETOWN, Co.	G-T
BATTLE CREEK, Neb.	B-C		GEORGETOWN, Del.	G-T
GRAND ISLAND, Neb.	G-I		GREENWOOD, Del.	G-W
NORTH PLATTE, Neb.	N-D		GEORGETOWN, D.C.	G-T
WEST POINT, Neb.	W-P		CLEARWATER, Fla.	C-W
ASBURY PARK, N.J.	A-P		RICHFIELD, Id.	R-F
ATLANTIC CITY, N.J.	A-C		SANDPOINT, Id.	S-P
JERSEY CITY, N.J.	J-C		GEORGETOWN, Ky.	G-T
LONG BRANCH, N.J.	L-B		NORTHFIELD, Minn.	N-F
NEW BRUNSWICK, N.J.	N-B		SCOTTSBLUFF, Neb.	S-B
OCEAN CITY, N.J.	O-C		SPRINGFIELD, Ohio	S-F
SEASIDE HEIGHTS, N.J.	S-H		GEORGETOWN, S.C.	G-T

b. Abbreviations to three letters
   Three words in print

NORTH LITTLE ROCK, Ark.	N-L-R
WEST PALM BEACH, Fla.	W-P-B
COUR-D'-ALENE, Id.	C-D-A
SALT LAKE CITY, Utah	S-L-C

All of the abbreviations listed in 1a and 1b are produced in neutral space slightly to the side of center. They have no movement in citation form other than that involved in the change from one handshape to the next.

2. Words in which the initial letter is followed by itself
   a. as the initial letter of the second word in
      i. two-word names
      ii. compound names
   b. in medial position
are abbreviated using the initial letter/handshape which nods very slightly, arcs slightly up and then down to the side.
   examples:
   a. i. BIG BEAR, Ca.
         STEAMBOAT SPRINGS, Co.
         BETHANY BEACH, Del.
         SANDY SPRINGS, Ga.
         SILVER SPRING, Md.
         ANN ARBOR, Mich.
         MOUNT MORRIS, Mich.
         FERGUS FALLS, Minn.
         POINT PLEASANT, N.J.
         WALLA WALLA, Wash.

   examples:
      ii. WILDWOOD, N.J.
          FAIRFIELD, Idaho

The present data suggest that there is one nod and one arc per medial letter which is identical to the initial letter.
   examples

   b. SHOSHONE, Id.
      FRANKFORT, Mich.   one medial letter identical
      OPELOUSAS, La.   to initial letter, one nod
      BRATTLEBORO, Vt.   and one arc.

      KANKAKEE, Ill.   two medial letters identical
                               to initial letter, two nods
                               and two arcs.

Certain other signs which utilize the nodding and arcing movement are limited to names with the initial letter F or H.

FAYETTEVILLE, N.C.
FINDLAY, Ohio
HARRISBURG, Pa.
HARRODSBURG, Ky.
HAGERSTOWN, Md.
HARRINGTON, Del.
HUNTINGTON, W.Va.

These signs utilize the nodding and arcing movement with the handshape of the initial letter of the word.

3. A very small group of abbreviations utilizes the first two letters of the printed word. The only abbreviations found so far which follow this rule are SYLACAUGA, Ala. (S-Y), SYRACUSE, N.Y. (S-Y), SPOKANE, Wash. (S-P), SPRINGFIELD, Ohio (S-P), and ELLENS-BERG, Wash. (E-L). At this time it appears that such abbreviations are limited to words with S or E in the initial position (see note 2).

   Battison (1978) describes a rule for the loan signs #SURE, #BUSY, #CLUB, and #COOL. In these signs the initial, one medial and final handshapes are preserved. Abbreviations for the following city names appear to follow a similar rule.

JUNEAU, Alaska	J-A-U
BRIDGEPORT, Conn.	B-P-T

We would like to thank Lewis Ballard, Robbin Battison, Dennis Cokely, and James Woodward for comments on earlier versions of these notes. Any errors are our own.

The signs contained in this text were collected from deaf individuals. However, no research was done on the origin or extent of use of specific signs. Usage may vary among deaf individuals, and the user should ascertain which sign is used in various situations. Future research may wish to investigate this area.

HJH

Notes

1. Rule 1 appears to handle LOS ANGELES quite well. The authors suggest that this sign is formed as if a signer were following rule 1 rather than as a derivation from the speech abbreviation *l-a*.

2. CHAMPAIGN, Ill. is not considered as an example of rule 3 due to the reduplication of the C-H which has been observed during data collection.

References

Battison, R. (1978). *Lexical borrowing in American Sign Language*. Silver Spring, Maryland, Linstok Press.

Doughter, S., Minken, M. and Rosen, L. (1980) *Signs for sexuality: A resource manual*. Seattle, Washington, Planned Parenthood.

Stokoe, W., Casterline, D. and Croneberg, C. (1965, 1976), *A dictionary of American Sign Language*. Silver Spring, Maryland, Linstok Press.

Wolfram, W., and Fasold, R. (1974), *The study of social dialects in American English*. Englewood Cliffs, New Jersey, Prentice-Hall.

Woodward, J. (1980a), *Signs of sexual behavior*. Silver Spring, Maryland, T.J. Publishers.
  (1980b) *Signs of drug use*. Silver Spring, Maryland, T.J. Publishers.
  (1980c). *Personal Communication*.

APPENDIX B

Signs and abbreviations which name cities in Canada and the U.S. were analyzed and compared to the general vocabulary of ASL and several signed English systems.

The following word groups have signs in American Sign Language or other sign systems which are identical.

SYMBOLS:

1 _____ shakes

2 _____ bobs

3 _____ nods

4 _____ circles

5 _____ nods, arcs to right, nods again or opens & closes moving to side

6 _____ wiggles down

7 _____ traces a 7

8a. _____ circles & touches temple
8b. _____ taps temple
8c. _____ circles near forehead

9 _____ arcs across chest

#10 _____ arcs down on palm

#11 _____ fingerspelled reduction

#12 _____ general vocabulary

For illustration purposes an A handshape will be used.

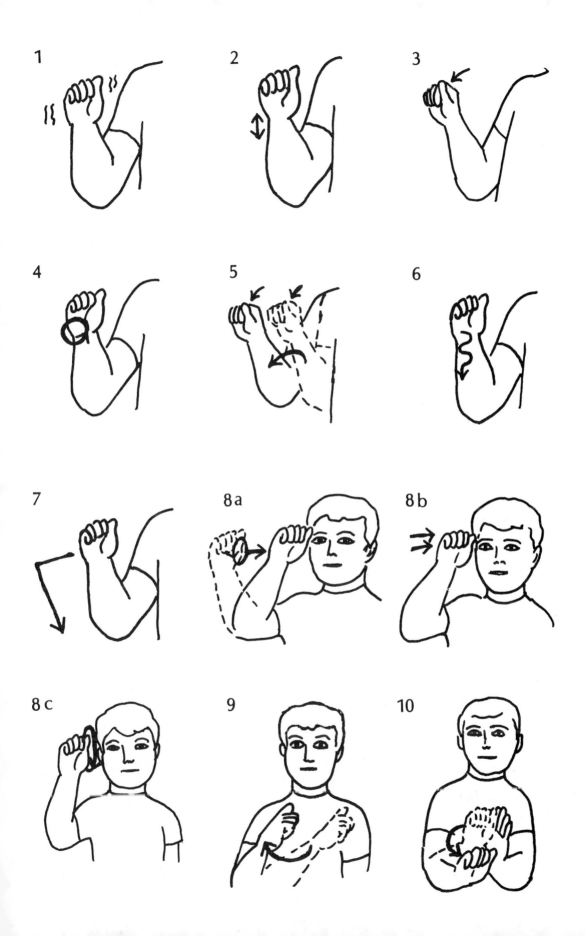

A #1
Alberta CAN
Amsterdam NY
Anderson IN
Anderson SC
Annapolis MD
Asheville NC
Augusta GA
Aurora IL

A #2
Alburquerque NM
Austin TX

A #5
Ann Arbor
A.A. (Assoc. of Arts degree)
Alcoholics Anonymous

A #7
Albany NY
Allentown NJ
Allentown PA
Alpena MI
Ahchorage AK
Austin TX

A #8b
Aberdeen SD
Abilene TX

A #9
Anniston AL
Atlanta GA

A #11
Albert Lea MN
Al

Alexandria LA
Alexandria VA
Alex

Asbury Park NJ
A & P store

Atlantic City NJ
Air conditioner

Auburn ME
a

A #12
Akron OH
rubber

Austin TX
any

Appleton WI
apple

Aurora CO
middle

Augusta ME
capitol
government
Tallahassee FL

B #1
Bangor ME
Bangor PA
Bellingham WA
Bellevue WA
Biloxi MS
Boise ID
Boulder CO
Brockton MA
Brooklyn NY

B #2
Berkeley CA
Birmingham AL
Bloomington IL
Bloomington IN
Boston MA
Brooklyn NY
Brooklyn OH

B #4
Bethlehem PA
Binghamton NY
Bloomington IL

B #5
Bethany Beach DE
Big Bear CA
Brattleboro VT

B #6
Beaverton OR
Birmingham AL
Buffalo NY

B #7
Bethlehem PA
Birmingham AL
Birmingham MI
Bluefield WV
Burlington VT
Burlington WI

B #11
Battle Creek MI
Battle Creek NB
British Columbia CAN
B.C. (time, A.D.)

B #12
Bear DE
bear
Big Bear CA
big bear

Brownsville TX
beer

Buffalo NY
buffalo

C #1
Calgary ALTA CAN
Centralia WA
Charleston SC
Charlotte NC

Chelsea VT
Chillawack BC CAN
Claymont DE
Columbia MD
Columbia MO
Columbus GA
Columbus OH
Cranston RI

C #5
Corpus Christi TX
Crescent City CA
carbon copy
cross country

C #6
Cleveland MS
climate

C #7
Carbondale PA
Chicago IL

C #9
Cedartown GA
Clarkston Ga
Cleveland OH
commission
committee
Congress

C #11
Council Bluffs IA
CB radio

Cedar Falls IA
Central Falls RI
captioned film
center field

Conneaut OH
Connecticut

Canoga Park CA
College Park GA
cerebral palsy

Cave Spring GA
Chehalis WA
Colorado Springs CO

Camden-Wyoming DE
Clearwater FL

C #12
Calgary ALTA CAN
cowboy

Canton OH
Cadillac

Caribou ME
chubby

Charleston WV
cousin

Charlottesville VA
capital

Cherokee NC
Indian

Columbia SC
cotton

Columbus ID
Jimmy Carter

Concord NH
capitol
Jimmy Carter

D #1
Danville KY
Decatur IL
Delavan WI
Denver CO
dormitory
Dover DE
Durham NC

D #2
Dayton OH
Denver CO

D #8b
Dallas TX
Diamond Head HI

D #11
Daytona Beach FL
Dewey Beach DE
decibel

Denham Springs LA
drug store

E #1
Easton MD
Easton PA
Ellensburg WA
Englewood CO
Euclid OH
Evansville IN
Everett WA

E #7
Emporia KS
Eugene OR

E #11
Eau Claire WI
Elk City OK

Edmonton ALTA CAN
El Dorado AR
education

Evanston WY
Europe

F #1
Florence SC
Framingham MA
Frederick MD
Fredericksburg VA
Fredericton, NB, CAN
Fremont NB

F #5
Fairfield ID
Fayetteville NC
Fergus Falls MN
Findlay OH
Frankfort MI
French fries

F #7
Fairbanks AK
Fayetteville NC
Flint MI

Fayetteville NC
film

F #12
Fairbault MN
pepper

Fond du Lac WI
Gerald Ford
federal

Frankfort KY
formula

G #4
Gainesville GA
Gaithersburg MD
Greenville SC

G #11
Green Bay WI
Grand Blanc MI

Glen Falls NY
Glenns Ferry ID
Grand Forks ND
Great Falls MT

Georgetown CO
Georgetown, Wash, D.C.
Georgetown DE
Georgetown SC
Georgetown TX
Georgetown NY

G #12
Gillette WY
shave

Gloversville NY
glove

Grand Mound IA
General Motors

Greenville NC
Greenwood SC
green

H #3
Hampton VA
Harrisonburg VA
Haverhill MA

H #5
Hagerstown MD
Harrington DE
Harrisburg PA
Harrodsburg KY
Honolulu HI
Huntingdon WV
hard-of-hearing

H #11
Hattiesburg MS
halfback

Hammond LA
ham

Hollywood CA
star

I #1
Ironton OH
Irving TX
insurance
independent

I #7
Independence MO
Indianapolis IN

I #12
Idaho Falls ID
if

Institute WI
St. Augustine FL
White Plains NY
institute
institution

Irving NJ
suppose

White Plains NY
liquor
whiskey

J #1
Jackson MS
Jacksonville AR
Joilet IL

J #11
Joilet IL
Jonesboro AR

Jefferson City MO
Jersey City NJ
Johnson City TN
Junction City KS

J #12
Jackson TN
Jacksonville FL
Jacksonville IL
job

K #1
Kearney NB
Kettering OH
Knoxville TN
ketchup
kitchen

K #11
Kansas City KS
Kansas City MO

K #12
Kingston PA
king

L #1
Lancaster PA
Laurel DE
Lawrence MA
Lewiston ID
Lincoln NB
Louisville KY

L #4
Lansdale PA
Lima OH
library

L #11
Lake Arthur LA
Lewiston-Auburn ME
Los Alamos NM
Los Angeles CA
Louisiana

Lafayette LA
Lafayette IN

Long Beach CA
Long Beach WA
Long Branch NJ

Lake Geneva WI
Lake George NY

Lincoln RI
Lubbock TX
Abraham Lincoln

Lenoir NC
Little Rock AR

Little Falls MN
left field

Long Island NY
long island

M #1
Manchester VT
Manitoba CAN
Miamisburg OH
Milford NH
Milford NJ
Morganton NC
Morristown TN

M #4
Manchester NH
Monday
Morganton NC

M #7
Manchester CT
Muskegon MI

M #8a
Madison WI
Montgomery AL

M #8b
Milledgeville GA
Mesquite TX
mind

M #9
Macon GA
Marietta GA
member

M #12
Manitoba CAN
man

Maryland
England

Menomonee Falls WI
mouse

Middletown DE
Middletown MD
Middletown OH
Middleville NY

Midland TX

Montpelier VT
politics

Montreal QUE CAN
middle

Mystic CN
mistake

N #1
Newark DE
Nicholville NY
Noblesville IN
Norfolk NB
Norfolk VA
Norristown PA

N #4
Nashua NH
Norristown PA

N #11
New Braunfels TX
New Brunswick NJ
North Bay ONT CAN

New Castle DE

North Carolina

New Haven CT
honest

New London CT
launder

New York
Yakima WA
Norfolk VA
nephew

Norfolk VA
niece

Northfield MN
Niagara Falls NY

New Plymouth ID
North Platte NB

O #1
Odessa DE
Ohio
Olympia WA
Omaha NB
Ontario CAN
Oregon
Orlando FL
Oshkosh WI
Owensboro KY

O #2
Oakland CA
Owatonna MN

O #4
Omaha NB
Ontario CAN
Oswego NY

O #5
Opelousas LA
Ottawa ONT CAN

O #7
Olathe KS
Opelousas LA
Ottawa ONT CAN
Owosso MI

O #11
Oak Creek WI
Ocean City MD
Ocean City NJ
Oklahoma City OK

O #12
Oak Ridge TN
or

Oglestown DE
too

P #1
Peoria IL
Petersburg VA
Pueblo CO
Portsmouth NH

P #3
Portland ME
Portland OR
Portsmouth OH
Providence RI

P #7
Philadelphia PA
Portsmouth NH
P #11
Pennsylvania
Port Angeles WA
Port Arthur TX
Prince Albert SASK CAN

Panama City FL
Pocomoke City MD

Pierre SD
politic

Port Moody BC CAN
p.m.

P #12
Pawtucket RI
false

Pittsburg KS
Pittsburgh PA

Plattsburg NY
benefit

Pontiac MI
Indian

Q #12
Queens NY
queen

R #1
Raleigh NC
Richmond ID
Richmond VA
Rome GA
Rutland VT

R #2
Racine WI
Riverside CA
Rochester MN
Rockford IL

R #4
Roanoke VA
rotate

R #7
Raleigh NC
Reading PA
Regina SASK CAN
Richmond IN
Richmond KY
Richmond VA
Riverside CA
Rochester NY

R #8b
Richardson TX
remind

R #11
Richfield ID
rightfield

R #12
Red Bank NJ
red bank

Red River NM
red river

Red Wing MN
red wing

Rome NY
doll

Rome NY
Greece

Rome NY
Rome Italy

S #1
Salem OR
Seattle WA
Smyrna DE
Spartanburg SC
Springfield VT
Statesville NC

S #4
Saturday
Savannah GA

S #5
Sandy Spring GA
shortstop
Shoshone ID
Silver Spring MD
social security
social studies
Steamboat Springs CO
Sunday school

S #6
Salisbury MD
season
Selma AL
semester

S #7
Scranton PA
semester
Springfield MA
Staunton VA
Sulphur OK

S #8c
Smithfield RI
Sweden

S #9
Savannah GA
Senate

S #10
Springfield IL
Springfield MO

St. Petersburg FL
Shreveport LA

S #11
Scottsbluff NB
South Bend IN

Sauk Centre MN
Sioux City IA
South Carolina
Swartz Creek MI

San Diego CA
South Dakota

San Francisco CA
Santa Fe NM
Santa Fe TX
Sioux Falls SD
Springfield MN
Springfield OH

Seaside Heights NJ
Shenandoah PA

Sandpoint ID
Spokane WA
Springfield OH
Sun Prairie WI

St. John NB CAN
St. Joseph MO

Sylacauga AL
Syracuse NY

S #12
St. Augustine FL
White Plains NY
Institute WI
institute
institution

Saratoga NY
compete

Sheboygan WI
sheep

Ship Rock NM
sail
ship

State College PA
state college

T #1
Tacoma WA
toilet

T #7
Talladega Al
Toledo OH
Topeka KS
Trenton NJ
Tulsa OK
Tucson AZ

T #9
Toledo OH
Toronto ONT CAN
Trenton NJ

T #11
Traverse City MI
total communication

Twin Falls ID
true-false

T #12
Tallahassee FL
Augusta ME

Temple TX
temple

U #4
Utica NY
use

V #1
Vancouver BC CAN
Vancouver WA
Vicksburg MS

V #11
Van Nuys CA
Viet Nam

Ville Platte LA
vice-president

V #12
Valentine NB
valentine

Vancouver BC CAN
van

Virginia Beach, VA
volleyball

W #1
Warwick RI
Winnipeg MAN CAN

W #2
Wausau WI
Wilmington DE
Worcester MA

W #4
Washington IN
Washington TX

W #5
Walla Walla WA
Weight Watchers
Woolworth's (store)

W #7
Wichita KS
Wilmington VT

W #11
West Harvard CT
Woodland Hills CA

West Point NB
Woodland Park CO
Woodland Park MI

W #12
Washington, D.C.
Washington IN
Washington State
George Washington

Watertown NY
Watertown SD

Westbrook ME
sour

White Bear Lake MN
white bear

White Bird ID
white bird
Whitehorse YUKON CAN
white horse

White Plains NY
Institute WI
institute
institution
St. Augustine FL

White Salmon WA
white salmon

Whitesburg KY
white

Williamsport PA
Poland

Y #3
Youngstown OH
yeah
yes

Y #12
Yakima WA
New York

Yellowknife NWT CAN
yellow knife

Yellowpine ID
yellow pine

INDEX

‡ indicates that the sign is identical to a sign used to name
another person, place or thing

‡Jackson TN
‡Jacksonville IL
‡Jacksonville AR
‡‡Jacksonville FL
Jefferson NY
‡Jefferson City MO
‡Jersey City NJ
Jersey Shore PA
‡Johnson City TN
Johnston RI
Johnstown PA
‡‡Joliet IL
‡Jonesboro AR
Junction City KS
Juneau AK
Kalamazoo MI
Kankakee IL
‡Kansas City KS
‡Kansas City MO
‡Kearney NB
Kenosha WI
Ketchikan AK
‡Kettering OH
‡Kingston PA
Kings Hill ID
Klamath Falls OR
‡Knoxville TN
Laconia NH
LaCrosse WI
‡Lafayette IN
‡Lafayette LA
Lake Arthur LA
Lake Arthur NM
Lake Charles LA
Lake Cruces NM
‡Lake Geneva WI
‡Lake George NY
Lake Placid NY
Lake Tahoe CA
Lakewood OH
‡Lancaster PA
Lander WY
‡Lansdale PA
Lansing MI
Lapeer MI
Laramie WY
Laredo TX
Las Vegas NV
Las Vegas NM
‡Laurel DE
Lava Hot Springs ID
‡Lawrence MA
‡Lenoir NC

Leavenworth KS
Lexington KY
‡Lewiston ID
Lewiston ME
Lewiston-Auburn ME
‡Lima OH
Lincoln IL
‡Lincoln NB
‡Lincoln RI
Lincoln City OR
‡Little Falls MN
‡Little Rock AR
Lock Haven PA
‡Long Beach CA
‡Long Beach WA
‡Long Branch NJ
‡Long Island NY
Lookout Valley TN
‡Los Alamos NM
‡Los Angeles CA
‡Louisville KY
‡Lubbock TX
Lynchburg VA
McAlester OK
‡Macon GA
‡Madison WI
‡Manchester CT
‡Manchester NH
‡Manchester VT
Manhattan NY
Manitou Springs CO
‡Marietta GA
Martinsville VA
Medford OR
Memphis TN
‡Menomonee Falls WI
Mesquite TX
Miami FL
‡Miamisburg OH
Michigan City IN
‡Middletown DE
‡Middletown MD
‡Middletown OH
‡Middletown NY
Middleville NY
Midland TX
‡Milford NH
‡Milford NJ
Milledgeville GA
Milwaukee WI
Minneapolis MN
Mobile AL
Monroe LA

Montevallo AL
‡Montgomery AL
Monticello AR
‡Montpelier VT
‡‡Morganton NC
‡Morristown TN
Mountain Home ID
Mount Morris MI
Mount Vernon WA
‡Muskegon MI
Muskogee OK
Myrtle Beach SC
‡Mystic CT
‡Nashua NH
Nashville TN
‡Newark DE
Newark NJ
‡New Braunfels TX
‡New Brunswick NJ
‡‡New Castle DE
‡New Haven CT
‡New London CT
New Orleans LA
‡New Plymouth
‡Newport RI
Newport News VA
New York City NY
‡Niagara Falls NY
‡Nicholville NY
‡Noblesville IN
‡Norfolk NB
‡‡‡Norfolk VA
‡‡Norristown PA
North Bend OR
‡Northfield MN
North Little Rock AR
‡North Platte NB
North Providence RI
‡Oak Creek WI
‡Oakland CA
‡Oak Ridge TN
‡Ocean City MD
‡Ocean City NJ
‡Odessa DE
Odessa TX
Ogletown DE
‡Oklahoma City OK
Okmulgee OK
‡Olathe KS
Old Forge NY
‡Olympia WA
‡‡Omaha NB
‡‡Opelousas LA

Oregon City OR
‡Orlando FL
‡Oshkosh WI
‡Oswego NY
Overland Park KS
‡Owatonna MN
‡Owensboro KY
‡Owosso MI
Palatka FL
‡Panama City FL
Pascagoula MS
‡Pawtucket RI
Pearl City HI
Pearl Harbor HI
Pensacola FL
‡Peoria IL
‡Petersburg VA
‡Philadelphia PA
Phoenix AZ
‡Pierre SD
Pine Bluff AR
‡Pittsburg KS
‡Pittsburgh PA
‡Plattsburg NY
Pocatello ID
‡Pocomoke City MD
Point Pleasant NJ
‡Pontiac MI
‡Port Angeles WA
‡Port Arthur TX
Port Huron MI
‡Portland ME
‡Portland OR
‡Portsmouth NH
‡Portsmouth OH
Portsmouth VA
Post Falls ID
Presque Isle ME
Princeton NJ
‡Providence RI
‡Pueblo CO
Puyallup WA
‡Queens NY
Quincy IL
‡Racine WI
‡‡Raleigh NC
Rapid City SD
‡Reading PA
‡Red Bank NJ
‡Red River NM
‡Red Wing MN
Rehoboth Beach DE
‡Richardson TX

‡Richfield ID
‡‡Richmond IN
‡Richmond KY
‡‡Richmond VA
‡‡Riverside CA
Riverton WY
‡Roanoke VA
‡Rochester MN
‡Rochester NY
‡Rockford IL
Rockmart GA
Rocky Mount NC
‡Rome GA
‡‡‡Rome NY
Romney WV
Russellville AR
‡Rutland VT
Sacramento CA
Saginaw MI
‡St. Augustine FL
‡St. Joseph MO
St. Louis MO
St. Paul MN
‡St. Petersburg FL
‡Salem OR
‡Salisbury MD
Salt Lake City UT
San Antonio TX
San Bernardino CA
‡San Diego CA
‡Sandpoint ID
‡Sandy Springs GA
San Fernando Valley CA
‡San Francisco CA
San Jose CA
San Marcus TX
Santa Barbara CA
‡Santa Fe NM
‡Saratoga NY
‡Sauk Centre MN
‡‡Savannah GA
Schenectady NY
‡Scottsbluff NC
‡Scranton PA
‡Seaside Heights NJ
‡Seattle WA
‡Selma AL
‡Sheboygan WI
‡Shenandoah PA
‡Ship Rock NM
‡Shoshone ID
‡Shreveport LA
‡Silver Spring MD

‡Sioux City IA
‡Sioux Falls SD
‡Smithfield RI
‡Smyrna DE
‡South Bend IN
‡‡Spartanburg SC
‡Spokane WA
Spring City PA
‡Springfield IL
‡Springfield MA
‡Springfield MN
‡Springfield MO
‡‡Springfield OH
‡Springfield VT
‡State College PA
Staten Island NY
‡Statesville NC
‡Staunton VA
‡Steamboat Springs CO
Stone Mountain GA
Sugar City ID
‡Sulphur OK
‡Sun Prairie WI
Sun Valley ID
‡Swartz Creek MI
‡Sylacauga AL
‡Syracuse NY
‡Tacoma WA
‡Talladega AL
‡Tallahassee FL
Tampa FL
Temple TX
Terre Haute IN
Texarkana AR
Thermopolis WY
‡‡Toledo OH
Toms River NJ
‡Topeka KS
‡Traverse City MI
‡‡Trenton NJ
‡Tulsa OK
Tuscaloosa AL
‡Tucson AZ
‡Twin Falls ID
University City MO
‡Utica NY
‡Valentine NB
Valley Forge PA
‡Vancouver WA
‡Van Nuys CA
‡Vicksburg MS
Victoria TX
‡Ville Platte LA

NOTES

OTHER PRODUCTS from
MODERN SIGNS PRESS, INC.

Basic Tools and Techniques
    Teaching and Learning Signing Exact English
    Student Workbook

Video Tapes
    Curriculum Tapes
        Beginning level – 14 lessons
        Rather Strange Stories (Intermediate level)

    Visual Tales (available in Signed English or ASL)
        The Father, The Son and The Donkey
        Village Stew
        The Greedy Cat
        The Magic Pot
        The House That Jack Built

    Signed Cartoons (available in Signed English or ASL)

Three Pigs	Three Bears	Casper	Animal Antics
Popeye	Raggedy Ann	Superman	Shipshape Shapes
Rudolph	Elmer & Bugs	Cinderella	Numbers
Daffy Duck	Bugs Bunny	Felix the Cat	

    Show and Tell Stories
        Series 1 – Brown Bear, Brown Bear...; and, This Is Me

    Informational Tapes
        Deafness the Hidden Handicap
        Growing Up with SEE

Children's Collection
    Coloring Books
        ABC's of Fingerspelling
        Sign Numbers

    Storybooks
        Talking Finger Series - Popsicles are Cold, At Grandma's House,
                Little Green Monsters, I was So Mad
        Jean's Christmas Stocking
        In Our House
        Be Happy Not Sad (two books including coloring workbook)
        Grandfather Moose (finger rhymes)

Greeting Cards
Color Your Own Cards (in both signs and words)
All Occasion
Birthday
Christmas

Special Products
Music In Motion
Pledge of Allegiance Poster
Signing Exact English in Spanish
Sport Signs
General Vocabulary
Football
Basketball
Baseball/Softball
Track and Field
Volleyball
Signs Everywhere
Signing English: Exact Or Not? (a collection of articles)
SEE What's Happening (a quarterly newsletter)
Fingerspeller & Fingernumber (software for Apple II Computers)
Signing Bears "Cookie" and "Honey"

More Yet To Come
CD Rom version of Signing Exact English
Cosmo Gets An Ear
More signed storybooks

FOR MORE INFORMATION ON OTHER PRODUCTS
MAIL – PHONE – FAX
TO REQUEST A FREE CATALOG

Modern Signs Press, Inc.

P.O. Box 1181
Los Alamitos, CA 90720

310/596-8548 V
310/493-4168 V/TDD
310/795-6614 FAX

NOTES

NOTES

NOTES

NOTES

NOTES

NOTES

NOTES

NOTES

NOTES